A Handful of Pearls

THE EPISTLE OF JAMES

By
Addison J. Eastman

THE WESTMINSTER PRESS
Philadelphia

BOOK DESIGN BY DOROTHY ALDEN SMITH

First edition

Published by The Westminster Press ®
Philadelphia, Pennsylvania

PRINTED IN THE UNITED STATES OF AMERICA

9 8 7 6 5 4 3 2 1

Library of Congress Cataloging in Publication Data

Eastman, Addison J
   A handful of pearls.

   Includes bibliographical references.
   1. Bible. N.T. James—Criticism, interpretation, etc. 2. Christian life—1960–   I. Title.
   BS2785.2.E17   227'.91'077   78–5797
   ISBN 0–664–24202–2

CONTENTS

PREFACE

The Christian church has a great treasure of incomparable worth in its literature. But it is an inheritance that each of us must rediscover in our own generation. The Epistle of James is part of that treasure which has not received the attention it deserves. This failure may be caused partly by the fact that today many people are generally confused about the authority of the Bible. But it may also be that the moral and ethical demands of the book of James are too painful, too demanding for our times.

When we read The Epistle of James seriously we have the feeling that we are not being serious enough. For there is a disturbing gap in most of us between what we say we believe and what we practice. And it is this gap which concerns James most.

To be sure, the style of the epistle is strange at first. It is a letter, but not the kind we get in the mail every day. It is a general letter, written for everyone to read. Furthermore, it consists of short sayings on various subjects without any discernible pattern. In this sense it reminds us of the book of Proverbs. It used to be that people likened this kind of writing to a string of pearls. But one looks in vain for a string that ties everything together in the book of James. So, as we shall see, it is much more accurate to compare the material in James to a handful of pearls.

As we read the epistle, we quickly realize that we are

handling precious gems. These vary greatly in size, shape, and luster. All of them relate pointedly to the practical problems of everyday living.

There is, for instance, the secret for dealing with disappointment and hardship. There is also a lot of good help for getting our priorities lined up in the right order. The common sins of the quick temper, the loose tongue, class discrimination, and the tendency to judge others all come in for a sharp look. James even deals with the sin of doing nothing! These are just a few of the pearls we'll be looking at more closely in this book.

In putting this volume together I have followed the order of subjects as they appear in the epistle. While a few passages might be clearer in one of the modern translations, I have used the Revised Standard Version throughout for the sake of consistency. The reader will profit by comparing the Scripture texts in various versions and translations.

The material in this book is addressed to those who have already found the Bible a lamp unto their feet. It is also for those who have, for whatever reason, decided that a book written nearly two thousand years ago can't possibly have anything interesting or important to say in our sophisticated and complex world. It is this latter group that will be most surprised. And if they read on with an open mind and heart, their whole way of looking at life could change.

No one can write on the diverse matters in The Epistle of James to the satisfaction of everyone. Many of the subjects are as controversial today as they were in A.D. 80. In writing this book, I have been influenced heavily by twelve years as a missionary in Burma, another twelve years in ecumenical work, and, most recently, seven years pastoring a suburban church in "mid-America." It was in this last situation that The Epistle of James took on new significance for me. As I tried to relate Biblical faith to the practical matters of everyday living, I became painfully aware of how far many of us have wandered from the path our Lord walked before us. At the same time, I was delighted to find a small group of people who were as eager as I was to learn more about the Bible and apply its message more radically to their common life. It is to these friends I owe the inspiration and encouragement to write this volume.

A.J.E.

CHAPTER 1

An Epistle of Straw?

One thing has always puzzled me. How can so many people claim they know the Bible and let some of the most exciting sections slip right by them unseen? It's like walking through the Grand Canyon with your eyes shut.

Take, for instance, The Epistle of James. It's hard to imagine anything more exciting. Yet ask the average person what he or she knows about the book, and you'll do well to get anything more than a shrug of the shoulders and a "care less" stare.

That's because many people approach the Bible as they do a large shopping center. They walk down the central mall and stop at a few of the large, well-known stores, but then rush right on past the smaller, less familiar shops. In this way they miss the book of James completely because it is so small. You can read its five chapters in about ten minutes. But diamonds and other gems are packed in very small boxes. The time has come for all of us to open the book of James and see what treasures it has been keeping for just such a time as this.

At first this may seem difficult, especially so, if you happen to be among those who remember that Martin Luther called James an "epistle of straw." The great Reformer's criticism was included in the last paragraph of his "Preface to the New Testament." There he made clear that his own preference was for the Gospel and the First Epistle of John, and the letters of Paul, particularly Romans, Galatians, and Ephesians, together with the First Epistle of Peter. He wrote: "They teach everything you need to know for your salvation. In comparison the Epistle of James is an epistle full of straw, because it contains nothing evangelical."[1]

Such objections are understandable. James says nothing at all about the death or resurrection of Christ. In fact, he mentions the Lord's name only twice. But does that really mean the book is not evangelical? It reminds me of my aunt who visited a church in our city and complained afterward: "It's too modernistic for me. The pastor only spoke the name of Christ once." Surely we must judge the Christian character of sermons and a great letter like James by something other than the number of times it uses the name of the Lord.

The truth is that if you read this letter carefully, you'll find it remarkably close to the spirit, as well as the actual words, of Jesus. For example, you'll find no fewer than twenty three references to, or quotations from, the Sermon on the Mount. More importantly, the major theme of the book ties in quite closely with Jesus' own warning:

Not every one who says to me, "Lord, Lord," shall enter the kingdom of heaven, but he who does the will of my Father who is in heaven. [Matt. 7:21]

In these words Jesus made a cutting distinction between people who merely talk religion and those who live their religion. James is concerned about the same contrast. He sounds his keynote in the words, "But be doers of the word, and not hearers only" [James 1:22].

All of us need such reminders today to help us avoid the common tendency to reduce religion to the use of certain familiar words and phrases. James has no time for playing such games. He views religion in such practical things as when to speak and when to keep your mouth shut. And he deals with these matters by using the most colorful imagery, as when he compares the importance of a person's tongue to the small rudder of a big ship, and when he likens the unstable person to a wave of the sea which is here one minute and gone the next.

To be sure, the book of James is different. In fact, its style is unlike any other book of the Bible. But it was a style of literature common enough in the first century. It is called paraenesis, and consists of short sayings without any discernible relationship between them. For this reason the Biblical scholar Edgar J. Goodspeed likened The Epistle of James to "a handful of pearls." In his *Introduction to the New Testament,* he writes:

> James is full of gems of religious thought. The question is: How are these related? The work has been compared to a chain, each link related to the one before it and the one after it. Others have compared its contents to beads on a string. Of course, the thought of the Christian life runs through it all, but that is too general a subject to give much coherence to contents so varied as these. Perhaps James is not so much a chain of thought, or beads on a string, as it is just a handful of pearls, dropped one by one into the hearer's mind.[2]

The writer of this important material identifies himself simply as "James, a servant of God and of the Lord Jesus Christ" [James 1:1]. That's literally all we know about him, so we're left guessing which of the three Jameses mentioned in the New Testament this one might be. Many have assumed him to be James the brother of our Lord, but the evident Greek style and language of the book make that assumption highly dubious. The brother of Jesus was a Galilean Jew whose first language was Aramaic. So the Greek-oriented writer of this letter must have been a different James. Or, there is a real possibility that the name of James was simply put on the book as a kind of patron. This was often done in the first century as a way of giving status to documents of all kinds.

In any case, let's take some delight in the fact we really don't have to know for sure who the author was. The important thing is to understand what he has to say, and even more important, to understand what God has to say to us through him.

One of the things we can learn from the very nature of the material itself has to do with how Christians and Jews relate to each other. This is because the book contains a great deal of Jewish material. It is a rather startling reminder that Christians and Jews were not always as far apart as they appear today. Our cultural separateness was described recently by my printer friend who grew up in Cleveland, Ohio. He said:

> All of us white kids lived in the main part of town, and we thought the whole country belonged to us. After all, our ancestors discovered it. Then, there were the half dozen black kids we saw in school and on the football field. And finally, there was the little "Jew boy" we never did get to know. His dad ran the clothing store, but none of us got down there very often.

So, the distance remains. But why should it? Rabbi Seymour Siegel, of the Jewish Theological Seminary of America, likens the relationship of the Jew and the Christian to that of an elder and a younger brother living in the same house. He asks, "How long can they ignore each other even if each has his own key?"[3]

The fact is that a writer of this epistle who called himself "a slave of the Lord Jesus Christ" considered Jewish material appropriate to Christian purposes. This shows how close the two communities were in the first century, which should come to us as no surprise. After all, the first Christians were Jews and remained so long after they became followers of Christ. Also, the Jewish scriptures formed the only Bible they had. And most important, Jesus, their Lord, was a Jew who never renounced his Jewishness. No wonder his disciples took for granted that one could become a Christian and still remain a Jew.

Surely the need is great in our time for rethinking this whole matter in the hope of overcoming prejudice on both sides. The change might come more quickly if we Christians, without compromising our convictions about the uniqueness of Christ, could begin to acknowledge how much we have in common with religious Jews and how much we are indebted to them. This little book of James is just such a reminder, since much of its material points to a high road down which Christians and Jews can walk proudly arm in arm.

But James is important today for still other reasons. The truth of the matter is that it deals head on with one of the most serious problems of our times—moral and ethical confusion. In the context of today's relaxed lifestyles it is important to hear James insist that in God's plan for the human race there are some things that are right and other things that are wrong. And these must not be confused. James followed closely in the footsteps of the prophet Isaiah, who said:

> Woe to those who call evil good
>   and good evil,
> who put darkness for light
>   and light for darkness,
> who put bitter for sweet
>   and sweet for bitter!
>
> [Isa. 5:20]

This is no cheap moralism. James is not saying, "Be morally upright, and you'll be a Christian." Rather, he is saying, "Be a real Christian and you'll be morally upright."

These are just a few of the many "pearls" we will be examining in the following chapters. To prepare yourself for an enriching experience, why not read all five chapters of James before you go to bed tonight? As you do, see if you can identify those sections which unite you with devout Jews. Then start thinking how you measure up to the book's high standard for everyday living.

THE LETTER
OF
JAMES

James, a servant of God and of the Lord Jesus Christ,
To the twelve tribes in the Dispersion:
Greeting.

2 Count it all joy, my brethren, when you meet
various trials, ³for you know that the testing of your
faith produces steadfastness. ⁴And let steadfastness
have its full effect, that you may be perfect and complete, lacking in nothing.

5 If any of you lacks wisdom, let him ask God, who
gives to all men generously and without reproaching,
and it will be given him. ⁶But let him ask in faith, with
no doubting, for he who doubts is like a wave of the
sea that is driven and tossed by the wind. ⁷, ⁸For that
person must not suppose that a double-minded man,
unstable in all his ways, will receive anything from the
Lord.

9 Let the lowly brother boast in his exaltation, ¹⁰and
the rich in his humiliation, because like the flower of
the grass he will pass away. ¹¹For the sun rises with its
scorching heat and withers the grass; its flower falls,
and its beauty perishes. So will the rich man fade away
in the midst of his pursuits.

12 Blessed is the man who endures trial, for when

he has stood the test he will receive the crown of life which God has promised to those who love him. [13]Let no one say when he is tempted, "I am tempted by God"; for God cannot be tempted with evil and he himself tempts no one; [14]but each person is tempted when he is lured and enticed by his own desire. [15]Then desire when it has conceived gives birth to sin; and sin when it is full-grown brings forth death.

16 Do not be deceived, my beloved brethren. [17]Every good endowment and every perfect gift is from above, coming down from the Father of lights with whom there is no variation or shadow due to change.[a] [18]Of his own will he brought us forth by the word of truth that we should be a kind of first fruits of his creatures.

19 Know this, my beloved brethren. Let every man be quick to hear, slow to speak, slow to anger, [20]for the anger of man does not work the righteousness of God. [21]Therefore put away all filthiness and rank growth of wickedness and receive with meekness the implanted word, which is able to save your souls.

22 But be doers of the word, and not hearers only, deceiving yourselves. [23]For if any one is a hearer of the word and not a doer, he is like a man who observes his natural face in a mirror; [24]for he observes himself and goes away and at once forgets what he was like. [25]But he who looks into the perfect law, the law of liberty, and perseveres, being no hearer that forgets but a doer that acts, he shall be blessed in his doing.

26 If any one thinks he is religious, and does not bridle his tongue but deceives his heart, this man's

[a] Other ancient authorities read *variation due to a shadow of turning*

religion is vain. [27]Religion that is pure and undefiled
before God and the Father is this: to visit orphans and
widows in their affliction, and to keep oneself un-
stained from the world.

CHAPTER 2

Your Friend Adversity

The Bible has a way of shocking us. You can be reading along quietly when all of a sudden an unexpected verse hits you like a jolt to the head and leaves you temporarily stunned.

James does this immediately after his brief greeting. In chapter 1, verse 2, he writes: "Count it all joy, my brethren, when you meet various trials."

Now that's a real switch! Most of us will do anything to avoid unpleasant experiences. In fact, we go along uncritically with the prevailing idea of our time that the ideal state of happiness is one of ease and unruffled comfort. And this assumption is carried over into every area of life. Some persons openly confess that they are interested in religion only if it can be a sort of tranquilizer.

But James waves the red flag on all this escapism, and in effect shouts: "Wait a minute. Instead of grumbling because you have problems, you should be grateful. After all, adversity can be your best friend."

Even on the purely secular level there is plenty of evidence that James was right. When you stop to think about it, hardships provide the challenges of life that are so essential to growth and achievement. This is probably why most of us will go out of our way to create problems if we don't have any. For instance, we'll take on new responsibilities which we know very well won't be easy, just to escape boredom. That may be the real explanation for mountain climbing. People climb mountains not just because they are there, but because mountain climbing is demanding; it is the raw material out of which achievement is made. It seems that God in his great wisdom has allowed hardship and suffering to be a part of human experience for strengthening character. It is a truism that most crises contain within them seeds of human growth. Not that God causes pain for anyone. But he takes pain and suffering, disappointments and defeat, and uses them for our own good.

Some of the most striking examples come from people who have used serious physical handicaps to attain true greatness. Take, for instance, Franklin Roosevelt. Polio was probably the greatest gift he ever received. According to those who knew him best, it instilled in him more sympathy for others and stimulated a greater sense of discipline. His wife, Eleanor, believed that without polio FDR might still have become President, but that he would not have accomplished what he did as President.

Or take Helen Keller, who was deaf, mute, and blind. The remarkable thing about Miss Keller is not merely that she accepted her afflications but rather that she used them. As a result, she found new and wonderful ways to perceive beauty around her. Indeed, she "saw" many things more clearly than you or I will ever see them because she was blind. If you have any doubts about this, consider a couple of paragraphs she once wrote in an essay for the *Atlantic* monthly:

Now and then I have tested my seeing friends to discover what they see. Recently I asked a friend, who had just returned from a long walk in the woods, what she had seen. "Nothing in particular," she replied.

"How was it possible," I asked myself, "to walk for an hour through the woods and see nothing worthy of note?" I who cannot see find hundreds of things to interest me through mere touch. I feel the delicate symmetry of a leaf.

I pass my hands lovingly about the smooth skin of a silver birch, or a rough, shaggy bark of a pine. In spring, I touch the branches of trees hopefully in search of a bird, the first sign of awakening nature after her winter's sleep. Occasionally, if I am very fortunate, I place my hand gently on a small tree and feel the happy quiver of a bird in full song.[4]

Helen Keller turned the handicap of blindness and deafness into her greatest asset.

Accidents too can often be used for our good. Take the case of Johann Gutenberg, who invented printing from movable type. It all started from a miserable accident. One day Gutenberg was putting the finishing touches on an intricate wood block for printing when his young apprentice ran by and carelessly knocked the precious block out of his hand. It fell to the floor and shattered into many pieces. Gutenberg probably said some strong words, but when he stooped to pick up the pieces, it suddenly flashed across his mind that he could use individual letters for printing just like the fragments he was picking up. It was this insight from a painful accident which led to the birth of modern printing.

Many other kinds of failure and disappointment have also brought their unexpected benefits.

Nathaniel Hawthorne, for instance, was not always a great writer. If you visit Salem, Massachusetts, you can walk through the old Customs House, where for years he held a responsible position. Then one day, as a result of party politics, Hawthorne was fired. At first he felt utterly defeated. But when his wife learned he had lost his job, she told him he would now have time to write the book he had always wanted to write. And so he wrote *The Scarlet Letter,* for which he will always have a place of renown in American literature. For Hawthorne, personal failure served to open new doors of opportunity.

So frequently is hardship an ingredient of creativity that some behavioral scientists are now saying no one succeeds in any field without serious obstacles or a handicap.

It's easy to believe, because so many new discoveries have come through the struggle to handle difficult problems. I was recently reading about Dr. William Beaumont, who was on the scene when a man was accidentally shot with a shotgun at close range. By all odds, the victim should have died. However, the opening in the man's stomach refused to heal. Beaumont tried everything, but the wound remained open. Finally, the doctor decided to use his problem for research. So the opening in the stomach of an otherwise healthy man became a kind of "window" through which Dr. Beaumont studied the digestive processes of the stomach. His discoveries revolutionized many medical theories and have benefited the whole human race. Difficulty became an advantage.

James saw this same principle long ago, and lifted it to the level of spiritual development. He tells us to be thankful for "trials," or hardships of all kinds, "for you know that the testing of your faith produces steadfastness" [James 1:3].

In Romans, Paul presents a similar statement of this important Christian insight:

> We rejoice in our sufferings, knowing that . . . endurance produces character. [Rom. 5:3–5]

The Epistle of First Peter is even more explicit. Referring to the Christian hope in Christ, he writes:

> In this you rejoice, though now for a little while you may have to suffer various trials, so that the genuineness of your faith, more precious than gold which though perishable is tested by fire, may redound to praise and glory and honor at the revelation of Jesus Christ. [I Peter 1:6–7]

James, like Peter and Paul, was writing to Christians. He was not saying that there are no real tragedies in life. He knew better. Neither did he promise that we will all be geniuses if we just suffer enough. But in many ways what he promises is even more important. For the goal of the Christian life is Christlike character. And here the point is that we should learn to welcome difficulties along life's way because they can strengthen our faith and help us become mature Christians—as James puts it, "perfect and complete, lacking in nothing" [James 1:4].

But how many people do you know who are able to give thanks for their hardships and setbacks? I have met very few. One is a former colleague, Dr. Melvin Schoonover. Mel was born with a rare bone disease called osteogenesis imperfecta. So was his daughter, Polly. Both have experienced dozens of fractures, long periods of hospitalization, and the pain of loneliness known by the handicapped. Both are confined to wheelchairs. Mel has written a book called *Letters to Polly: On the Gift of Affliction.* In it he tries to explain to his daughter the liberation he found, not simply in spite of his affliction, but to a very real extent just because of it.

In one of the letters he proves what The Epistle of James has to say about hardships. He writes:

I am not "putting you on" when I say that I consider myself a very fortunate, even privileged person. That is why I have decided to write you these letters . . . to share some things with you that will at least preserve your hope that the end of the struggle is not despair, but hope and joy.[5]

Why not close this book for a minute and think of your most difficult problem. Let your faith move in on it until you can believe that God in his great love can help you to turn that problem into a great advantage. Imagine some of the ways he may want to do this. Write them down. Then begin to watch for ways God is trying to lead you. This could be the beginning of a new way of life!

CHAPTER 3

Money Can Fool You

How would you like to be a millionaire? It's a dream as American as big cars. But it can be dangerous.

We usually think of wealthy people living in beautiful mansions, riding in big limousines driven by uniformed chauffeurs, always happy and without any problems. But The Epistle of James doesn't see it that way at all. Instead, the writer says the rich should "weep and howl" for the miseries that are theirs. Three prominent kinds of wealth in that day were clothing, grain, and precious metal. So James says in ch. 5:2–3: "Your garments are moth-eaten. Your gold and silver have rusted." To be sure, James wasn't writing primarily for the rich. If you read his letter carefully, you'll see that the author was writing to people on the lower rungs of the economic ladder. But, like the poor everywhere, they were apparently envious of the well-to-do. I can imagine them saying to one another, "If we just had enough land, jewelry, and cash in the mattress, all our problems would be solved."

To such mistaken souls of that day, and to all of us, James shouts a clear warning. He says material wealth is not at all what it appears to be, and that if we're not careful, that attitude can get us into a pile of trouble.

For instance, he points out that material things can very easily mislead us. They give us a false sense of security. Sure, if you're rich, you can buy all kinds of goods and services, but this makes it easy to forget that life is brief and that you can't take any of your wealth with you. So, three times in his short letter James reminds us that the rich don't live any longer than anybody else. In the fourth chapter, he says they are like "a mist that appears for a little time and then vanishes" [ch. 4:14]. And in the first chapter, he compares them to flowers of the field, which are here one day and gone the next.

> Like the flower of the grass he [the rich] will pass away. For the sun rises with its scorching heat and withers the grass; its flower falls, and its beauty perishes. So will the rich man fade away in the midst of his pursuits. [James 1:10–11]

All of us who are Americans need this same kind of reminder, for we live on the Park Avenue of the world, where it is very easy to forget what's most important. Material wealth has a way of whispering sweet promises in our ears which it can never fulfill.

The writer of Ecclesiastes told the truth when he wrote:

> As [man] came from his mother's womb he shall go again, naked as he came, and shall take nothing for his toil, which he may carry away in his hand. [Eccl. 5:15]

In other words, "You can't take it with you." But still we try! It's reported that a wealthy man specified in his will that $10,000 of his money should be put beside him when he was buried. His brother was the executor. A month after the funeral, the lawyer asked the brother if the terms of the will had been followed. "Yes," he said. "It was tough, but I did it." The lawyer asked, "What denominations of bills did you use?" "Well," replied the man, "the bills turned out to be too bulky, so I wrote out a personal check and put it in my brother's casket."

It's easy to get the idea that we can take it with us. But that's not all. Material possessions have a way of possessing us. The person with a lot of money can easily become enslaved by it. That must have been what happened to the rich young ruler who came to Jesus one day asking about eternal life. Jesus loved the young man and told him to go and sell what he had and give it to the poor. Instead, the young man went away sorrowful. He was very rich, and his wealth had become his master. [Luke 18:18–30.]

We are talking now about the dangers of getting rich. Lest you think this doesn't apply to you, let's take a minute to note that you don't have to be a millionaire to be materialistic. Remember, it's not money, but the love of money that the Scripture says is the root of all evil. And one who has little of this world's goods can be ruled by things as surely as the millionaire. A young man whose family came to this country from Yugoslavia said: "My dad came over here from the old country with nothing but the shirt on his back. He was determined to get more money than his two brothers. And the almighty dollar finally killed him."

Some Asian visitors to the United States rightly deplore the materialism of our culture, and go on to tell us that the people in their homeland are more "spiritual." This is often a false generalization in which poverty is equated with spirituality. The two are by no means the same. The poor farmer in India, whose income is less than $100 a year, can be as possessed by material concerns as his American brother who makes $100 a day. You see, it isn't how much you have, but what rules your life, that counts.

That much is pretty obvious, but here's another angle. Material wealth is dangerous because it frequently divides people from each other. I know a family that had to call off its family reunion last year because three of the four brothers weren't on speaking terms. Their mother had died during the year and each thought he should have received a larger share of the family estate.

Sudden wealth has also been known to break up marriages. For instance, Robert S. Brown won the Maryland

State Lottery in 1974 for a prize of $50,000 a year. When his wife heard the news, instead of being happy, she said, "You shouldn't have won; it's going to ruin our marriage." Sure enough, it did. Within a year, the Browns were separated and have since obtained a divorce. In an article in *Family Circle,* Mr. Brown laments, "We just couldn't communicate after the money came."[6] You see, material possessions are like that. They have a way of building walls around people.

But more than that, and most serious, riches are dangerous because they often separate people from God. It's easy for the wealthy person to forget God, because he assumes he is all-sufficient, that with his riches he can buy anything. He forgets that one of our nation's richest citizens, Howard Hughes, died the death of a pauper. One of the doctors who did the postmortem said simply that he died of neglect. Happiness is not to be equated with prosperity, rather it is the by-product of right living in an open, honest relationship with our heavenly Father. We all know that, yet the advertising industry continues to mislead us. I recently received a letter from my bank which read:

> It's been our experience that nothing lifts one's spirit quite like a healthy infusion of fresh cash. . . . Maybe the time is ripe for our Spirit Lifter Loan? . . . Let's talk about what it will take to lift your spirit. I think you will find our terms reasonable, our people agreeable, and our advice sound.

In contrast, television's emcee Merv Griffin recently interviewed a multimillionaire oilman from Texas. The highlight of the conversation came unexpectedly when Merv asked the millionaire, "How much money does it take to make a person happy?" The answer came back swiftly but sadly, "Always, just a little bit more."

Wasn't this the underlying point of our Lord's parable about the rich man who built bigger barns [Luke 12:16–21]?

There was nothing wrong with the barns. But there was something tragically wrong with the builder. He had lost perspective, and his great wealth had separated him from God.

So, all in all, wealth can give you a false security, can become your master, can separate you from your brothers, and it can separate you from God.

In the light of all these dangers, is it any wonder that Jesus said, "It is easier for a camel to go through the eye of a needle than for a rich man to enter the kingdom of God" [Matt. 19:24]?

Furthermore, we can now see more clearly why our Lord said, "Do not lay up for yourselves treasures on earth, where moth and rust consume and where thieves break in and steal" [Matt. 6:19]. The truth is, it is foolish to put your trust in material things which can do so much damage and provide no lasting security.

What is the alternative? Jesus said, "But lay up for yourselves treasure in heaven" [Matt. 6:20]. And what does that mean? We all know how to lay up earthly treasure [though we can't seem to do it], but we haven't given much thought to how one goes about accumulating treasures in heaven. Doesn't it come down finally to personal trust in God and taking to heart the promise that nothing can separate us from his love—ever? That's the treasure no amount of money can buy, which moth and rust cannot corrupt, and which thieves cannot break through and steal.

The Christian walks through life as a pilgrim. He uses material things, but he holds on to them lightly. He knows well they are never his. He is only a steward of them and seeks to use them for God's glory. We can never be the permanent holder of things.

So we all need to reexamine our goals in life. What do you want most? Really. Are you basically a materialist? You say, "No, the spiritual dimensions of life are the most important." And this leads to another question. Ask yourself: "Does my present life-style adequately reflect my true priorities? If the spiritual side of life is important, how can I show it?"

CHAPTER 4

The Battle Within

Tom is a tall sixteen-year-old, well known at school for his brilliant track record. His parents were shocked, however, when Tom came home the other night drunk. The next morning his dad asked, "Why? Why did you do it?" And Tom answered as honestly as he knew how, "I really don't know." But his dad persisted. "You know better," he said. "We've brought you up in a good Christian home. Whatever made you do such a thing?" This time the boy tried a completely different tack. He said simply, "I guess the devil made me do it." And there ended the critical conversation.

Debbie is an attractive twenty-five-year-old who has a master's degree in music. As a college student she was converted to Christian faith through the Children of God movement. A couple weeks ago Debbie was offered a job that combined singing with some tutoring. It seemed tailor-made to her talents and training, and she needed work badly. So she promised Mr. Jenks she would call him by 8:00 P.M. Tuesday if she decided to take the job. But the day came and went with no call from Debbie. A week later her mother found out she had lost the job because she didn't call. So her mom asked, "Debbie, why on earth didn't you call the man as you promised?" Debbie shrugged her shoulders and answered: "I really don't know, but my life is completely in God's hands. If he had wanted me to have that job, he would have seen to it that I got it."

Tom and Debbie don't even know each other, but they are both ducking out on responsibility for their own behavior. The only difference is that Tom is blaming the devil and Debbie is blaming God. In both cases, religion is used as an escape from accountability. This is a tendency common among Christians, but totally alien to the faith of the Bible.

In contrast to this kind of escapism, the writer James says:

Let no one say when he is tempted, "I am tempted by God"; for God cannot be tempted with evil and he himself tempts no one; but each person is tempted when he is lured and enticed by his own desire. Then desire when it has conceived gives birth to sin; and sin when it is full-grown brings forth death. [James 1:13–15]

Here James pushes us all back where we have to accept responsibility for our own behavior. This is good Christian theology. Biblically, human desires stand under the judgment of God, and man is accountable for self-discipline. The word "desire" is used in the Scripture to denote an intense assertion of self-will. The New English Bible translates the word as "lust," but it is much too restrictive to equate desire with sexual needs, as we usually do when we use that word. The way Biblical writers use the term "desire," it is morally neutral. It is only when desire is fulfilled in wrong ways that it becomes evil. Unlike Buddhism, Christianity makes no attempt to get rid of desire, but rather to channel it in right directions. The Four Noble Truths taught by the Buddha are:

1. Existence involves suffering.
2. The cause of suffering is desire.
3. The way to rid oneself of suffering is to rid oneself of desire.
4. To rid oneself of desire, one must follow the Eightfold Path.

Christmas Humphreys, in his book on Buddhism, explains further that in Buddhism desire is "the lust of the flesh, the lust of life (existence) and the love of this present world."[7]

In contrast, the Biblical writers teach us how to handle our God-given desires in constructive and responsible ways. This is a lifelong task. The apostle Paul apparently had trouble with it to his dying day. He wrote: "I do not do the good I want, but the evil I do not want is what I do. . . . Who will deliver me from this body of death?" Then he adds, "Thanks be to God . . ." [Rom. 7:19, 24, 25]. There is victory, even our faith.

We've been looking at desire through theological glasses. It may also help to view the matter psychologically. Psychologists point out that all of us are born with a long list of needs, or what they call drives, and part of growing up is learning to handle these drives in a responsible manner.

Some of these needs are primarily biological, like the need for oxygen and food. Others are emotional or psychic, like the need to love and to be loved. In lower forms of life the elemental drives are cared for automatically, but in human life they are left to personal choices. Thus, a person may decide to go without food for what he considers a higher goal. This is in keeping with our Scripture, which is built on the premise that personal morality depends on how we handle our basic drives. Without the discipline of wise choices, desires run wild and lead to destruction.

One example of what can happen is cited by James in the fourth chapter of his letter:

> What causes wars, and what causes fightings among you? Is it not your passions that are at war in your members? You desire and do not have; so you kill. And you covet and cannot obtain; so you fight and wage war. [James 4:1–2]

Whether these verses are literal references to military conflict or a simple way of describing church fights, individual and corporate selfish desire is at the bottom of it all.

In these verses James is telling us some important things

about ourselves. First, he is saying, "You are free." This is basic to anything else we may say about ourselves.

Indeed it takes us back to our very origins. The Genesis story makes it unmistakably clear that the first pair, Adam and Eve, possessed the ability to make choices, including the frightful one of whether to say yes or to say no to their maker.

It was as though God had placed them in the garden and said: "it's up to you. You are now free to make of life what you want it to be. You can fill it with meaning and joy. Or you can destroy it with guilt and emptiness. You are even free to reject your freedom."

Then the poet uses the figures of forbidden fruit and an evil serpent to bring the issue of human freedom into sharpest focus. God gave Adam and Eve clear instructions, but left it completely up to them to decide how they would respond. Unfortunately, they chose not to accept their God-given limitations. It wasn't that they were so hungry for apples. Rather, the serpent had said, "When you eat of it your eyes will be opened, and you will be like God." [8]

So, freely they ate! And later when God asked what they had done, Adam blamed Eve, and Eve blamed the serpent. But the central point of the incident cannot be missed. The first pair were everyman and everywomen in their innate freedom to decide how they would respond to the givens of life.

Sadly enough, many people never got started right in life, because they never understood, or at least never accepted, the fact of their own freedom. And like Tom and Debbie, they continue to neglect or ignore their own ability to choose. Many people today would rather see their fate determined by Aquarius or Leo, their DNA, or their early toilet training—anything but by their own choices. James, on the other hand, makes it clear that we are free to become what we know we ought to be.

The other thing James tells us about ourselves is that we

are responsible. This is simply the other side of freedom, like cause and effect. If our choices are really our own, as we know in our better moments they are, then we also know we are responsible for how we make these choices. It simply isn't possible to be free without being accountable any more than it is possible to see without having eyes. So many people get hung up these days because they want to be free to do as they please, but they don't want to be responsible for the consequences.

What would it mean to one's identity if one were in no way accountable for one's behavior? Such a person would quickly go to pieces, feeling that no one cared. Unless others take us seriously, ultimately we would not be able to take ourselves seriously. One wonders if this is not at least a part of what has happened to many of our youth today who have no clear ideas about right and wrong, and consequently no sense of responsibility. A feeling of guilt is surely a miserable thing, but even a guilty conscience sharpens one's awareness of personhood.

In the musical *West Side Story,* there is a song that usually brings laughter to the audience. It is called "Gee, Sergeant Krupke," and it is sung by one of the street gangs. The delinquent boys who sing it have been through all kinds of modern analysis and have been told they are not boys, but are just helpless victims of a changing community. Their song to the neighborhood policeman makes fun of those who so easily excuse them. The final verse ends with a statement that it is not a question of being misunderstood:

> "Deep down inside him he's no good."

And then all the boys join in the chorus:

> We're no earthly good;
> The best of us is no damn good.[9]

This is more than just humor. These boys aren't about to give up their identity and sense of meaning in life. So they insist they are responsible human beings. They won't let anyone explain them away as products of an unfortunate environment. They prefer to be responsible and judged "no good" than become nonentities.

Here again the message of James is fundamental. Each of us is given a basic set of drives or desires and each of us is accountable for what we do with them. It is in this accounting, good or bad, that we discover who we are.

So let us look again at our lives and see if we can honestly avoid the mistake of Tom and Debbie in blaming either God or the devil for our moral failures. Each of us is free to choose and each of us is accountable.

CHAPTER 5

Count to Ten

Know this, my beloved brethren. Let every man be quick to hear, slow to speak, slow to anger, for the anger of man does not work the righteousness of God. [James 1:19–20]

Here James is telling us that a hot temper is completely out of place in the life of an intelligent, mature Christian. As he wrote he may have had in mind the familiar words of Jesus about anger in the Sermon on the Mount:

You have heard that it was said to the men of old, "You shall not kill; and whoever kills shall be liable to judgment." But I say to you that every one who is angry with his brother shall be liable to judgment; whoever insults his brother shall be liable to the council, and whoever says, "You fool!" shall be liable to the hell of fire. [Matt. 5: 21–22]

In these and other passages, the Scripture is clear and consistent in teaching that undisciplined anger no more fits the Christian life than pork fits the Jewish diet. The apostle Paul lists anger in his catalog of sins with what he calls the "works of the flesh." Actually, these lists, such as in II Cor. 12:12, Gal. 5:19–21, and Col. 3:8, describe the life-style of pagans, and deal with habits not to be found among Christians who have "put on Christ."

Yet as clear as the Bible is on this matter, many people, even some Christians, still have the idea that a strong temper isn't all that bad. They think it's better than repressing their feelings. So they excuse their violent outbursts with the comment, "At least I get it off my chest." Well, we need to be clear there's nothing Christian about that. To the contrary, Scripture teaches that it's the fool who blows his top when he is irritated. The wise man, in contrast, directs his feelings of displeasure into more constructive channels. It's not that the hot-tempered person has any more feeling, than the silent type, or even stronger feelings. He just wears them on his tongue! It's the difference between exploding a can of gasoline in one big dangerous bang or pouring it into an engine where it burns slowly and where the energy is used to generate power.

In the Old Testament it is the book of Proverbs which has the most to say about the short fuse. Here are some of the gems:

> He who is slow to anger has great understanding,
>   but he who has a hasty temper exalts folly.
>   [Prov. 14:29]

> A hot-tempered man stirs up strife,
>   but he who is slow to anger quiets contention.
>   [Prov. 15:18]

> A fool gives full vent to his anger,
>   but a wise man quietly holds it back.
>   [Prov. 29:11]

And here's one my mother used to quote whenever I argued with my brother (which was often):

> A soft answer turns away wrath,
>   but a harsh word stirs up anger.
>
>   [Prov. 15:1]

Finally, consider this one which puts the whole thing in perspective:

He who is slow to anger is better than the mighty,
and he who rules his spirit than he who takes a city.
[Prov. 16:32]

Self-control is better than political or military authority. In fact, a man may be in a position to exercise power over many, but if he can't rule his own temper, he's a washout. For how can a man handle others when he isn't able to handle himself? When the boss gets mad, the institution is in serious trouble.

But now back to James. He writes: "Be quick to hear, slow to speak, slow to anger, for the anger of man does not work the righteousness of God" [James 1:19-20].

These words are perhaps best understood when we remember that there was no New Testament in those early days and that congregations depended on traveling missionaries for the preaching of the gospel. In this situation, James was saying: "To get the greatest benefit from such preaching, you should always be eager to hear, reluctant to interrupt, and slow to lose your temper when you don't agree with what is said."

That is still good advice! But today the words have even broader implications—especially the last part: "for the anger of man does not work the righteousness of God."

Why not? What's really wrong with losing your temper and letting it all hang out? Well, first and most obvious, somebody usually gets hurt. Flying into a rage may give momentary release to your feelings, but it tramps all over the feelings of others. In this regard, the quick temper is very self-centered behavior. It is just the opposite of consideration for the feelings of others.

You may rationalize: "Well, once I get it out of my system, it's all over. I don't hold any grudges." Perhaps so, but where is the regard for the other person? Some of the hurt you have done may be irreparable. We say such awful things when we're mad. That must be why Thomas Jefferson used to advise: "When angry, count ten before you speak; if very angry, an hundred."[10] (You can forget Mark Twain's parody on those words. He said, "When angry, count four; when very angry, swear.")[11]

Another thing wrong with losing your temper is that it's childish. Literally! It's the way the youngster gets what he or she wants. At least it gets attention, and often more than that. Like last week in the supermarket. A four- or five-year-old boy was whining. His mother was ignoring him, but finally turned and said harshly: "No, you're too old to ride in the cart. Now you just walk like a little gentleman." Well, you guessed it. The "little gentleman" sat down in the middle of the aisle and started to yell. But not for long, because mama came running and said, "All right, all right, just this once." And she lifted the victorious child up on the cart.

No wonder the child's rule is, "When everything else fails, throw a good temper tantrum." Some people carry this same flight plan right over into their forties and fifties. You notice I didn't say "into adulthood," because these are the folks who never quite become adults. You know some of these folks who are really just spoiled children. The temper tantrum, or flying off the handle, is one of the sure signs such persons never grew up. They are still trying the tricks that got them attention when they were four years old. The apostle Paul said, "When I became a man, I put away childish things" [I Cor. 13:11]. But obviously, a lot of people haven't. James would have agreed with the Greek poet Homer, who wrote almost one thousand years B.C.: "You ought not to practice childish ways, since you are no longer that age."[12]

Still another reason a violent temper is bad is that it is usually a cover-up for some other weakness. It is not a mark of strength, but rather a sure sign that something is lacking. The Chinese have a proverb that says, "The man who is losing the argument strikes the first blow." Did you ever notice it? Usually the persons who fly into a rage are the ones who have lost the argument and no longer have any rational tools at their command. At least they don't know how to use them. Therefore, they blow their tops and in doing so show how really weak they are. At this point an old word of caution may be in order. That is, before you give someone a piece of your mind, be sure you have a piece you can spare.

Finally, and most important, James tells us that man's anger cannot achieve the purposes of God. He doesn't explain why. By its very nature a fiery temper feeds on contempt for the other person. Some studies have been done with small schoolchildren which show that children seldom get angry with a teacher they really care for. They are too eager to please and to be liked. It is the teacher they despise who makes them mad—even though the two teachers insist on the same requirements.

In the light of this finding, will you agree that the only real cure for a bad temper is a change of attitude toward other persons? As long as you can say, "I don't care what anybody thinks," you can and will go right on blowing your stack and maiming people in the process. But this is where religion comes in. If the love of God is shed abroad in your heart, you will care very much about other people and their feelings. And you'll find that love will make temper tantrums as unnecessary as the playpen.

For as the apostle Paul put it, "Love is patient and kind; . . . is not arrogant or rude. . . . Love does not insist on its own way; it is not irritable or resentful" [I Cor. 13:4–5].

That's the alternative to a wild temper. So, "Know this, my beloved brethren. Let every man be quick to hear, slow to speak, slow to anger, for the anger of man does not work the righteousness of God" [James 1:19–20].

Now take a few minutes to review the main points of this

chapter. An uncontrolled temper is completely out of place for the Christian. It is unacceptable to God, and a mark of weakness. Do you really believe this? Then draw up your own plans to do something about it. The rewards will show up immediately.

THE LETTER
OF
JAMES

My brethren, show no partiality as you hold the faith 2
of our Lord Jesus Christ, the Lord of glory. [2]For if a man
with gold rings and in fine clothing comes into your
assembly, and a poor man in shabby clothing also
comes in, [3]and you pay attention to the one who
wears the fine clothing and say, "Have a seat here,
please," while you say to the poor man, "Stand
there," or, "Sit at my feet," [4]have you not made distinctions among yourselves, and become judges with
evil thoughts? [5]Listen, my beloved brethren. Has not
God chosen those who are poor in the world to be rich
in faith and heirs of the kingdom which he has promised to those who love him? [6] But you have dishonored the poor man. Is it not the rich who oppress you,
is it not they who drag you into court? [7]Is it not they
who blaspheme the honorable name which was in-
voked over you?

8 If you really fulfil the royal law, according to the
scripture, "You shall love your neighbor as yourself,"
you do well. [9]But if you show partiality, you commit
sin, and are convicted by the law as transgressors.
[10]For whoever keeps the whole law but fails in one
point has become guilty of all of it. [11]For he who said,
"Do not commit adultery," said also, "Do not kill." If

you do not commit adultery but do kill, you have become a transgressor of the law. ¹²So speak and so act as those who are to be judged under the law of liberty. ¹³For judgment is without mercy to one who has shown no mercy; yet mercy triumphs over judgment.

14 What does it profit, my brethren, if a man says he has faith but has not works? Can his faith save him? ¹⁵If a brother or sister is ill-clad and in lack of daily food, ¹⁶and one of you says to them, "Go in peace, be warmed and filled," without giving them the things needed for the body, what does it profit? ¹⁷So faith by itself, if it has no works, is dead.

18 But some one will say, "You have faith and I have works." Show me your faith apart from your works, and I by my works will show you my faith. ¹⁹You believe that God is one; you do well. Even the demons believe—and shudder. ²⁰Do you want to be shown, you shallow man, that faith apart from works is barren? ²¹Was not Abraham our father justified by works, when he offered his son Isaac upon the altar? ²²You see that faith was active along with his works, and faith was completed by works, ²³and the scripture was fulfilled which says, "Abraham believed God, and it was reckoned to him as righteousness"; and he was called the friend of God. ²⁴You see that a man is justified by works and not by faith alone. ²⁵And in the same way was not also Rahab the harlot justified by works when she received the messengers and sent them out another way? ²⁶For as the body apart from the spirit is dead, so faith apart from works is dead.

CHAPTER 6

Who's Who in the Kingdom

The New Testament is a revolutionary document! Not that it promotes violence, but in the sense that it so often upsets our commonly held assumptions.

For instance, take the idea of who is important and who isn't. Almost every culture, in all periods of history, has tended to rate people along economic lines: the rich at the top of the ladder, the poor at the bottom rung. Such classifications are widespread, and sometimes get smuggled into the Christian church. But the New Testament writer, James, tells us pointedly that such distinctions are sinful and have to go. He writes:

My brethren, show no partiality as you hold the faith of our Lord Jesus Christ, the Lord of glory. For if a man with gold rings and in fine clothing comes into your assembly, and a poor man in shabby clothing also comes in, and you pay attention to the one who wears the fine clothing and say, "Have a seat here, please," while you say to the poor man, "Stand there," or, "Sit at my feet," have you not made distinctions among yourselves, and become judges with evil thoughts? Listen, my beloved brethren. Has not God chosen those who are poor in the world to be rich in faith and heirs of the kingdom which he has promised to those who love him? But you have dishonored the poor man. . . .

If you really fulfil the royal law, according to the scripture, "You shall love your neighbor as yourself," you do well. But if you show partiality, you commit sin, and are convicted by the law as transgressors." [James 2:1–9]

James was not alone in denouncing such snobbishness. The apostle Paul touched the thing at its center when he wrote to masters and slaves in the sixth chapter of Ephesians. He told the masters to stop threatening their slaves, "knowing that he who is both their Master and yours is in heaven, and that there is no partiality with him" [Eph. 6:9].

Quite obviously, there must have been some social problems in the first-century church. At least some members of the congregation had become too class conscious. They were rolling out the red carpet for the rich and letting the poor people in rags sit on the floor. All of that was many centuries ago, but we would be less than honest if we claimed that the church in our day is completely free from such things. One doesn't need a Ph.D. in sociology to figure out that many of our churches are in effect class churches, simply reflecting the divisions of society at large. As any pastor can tell you, it is very hard to integrate a blue-collar worker into a white-collar church, to say nothing of integrating a black person into a white congregation. So this passage from James speaks directly to all of us who call ourselves Christians.

It is surprising to learn that some scholars have discounted these particular verses of James as having little to do with Christian faith. For instance, Burton Scott Easton in the exegesis section of *The Interpreter's Bible* [Vol. 12, p. 35] writes: "The section as a whole may unhesitatingly be pronounced pre-Christian."[13]

Such a judgment becomes difficult to understand if you relate the words of James to what Jesus stood for and what he taught about social snobbery. The truth is that our Lord went out of his way to challenge the whole idea of a social ladder in his day. In fact, he often shocked people by reversing the order, the rich at the bottom and the poor at the top. He made a despised Samaritan the hero of his story about human need. And in his home church at Nazareth he ended his sermon by recalling the work of the ancient prophets Elijah and Elisha. He reminded his townspeople that though there were many widows in Israel, Elijah was sent to none of them, but instead to a foreigner, the widow Zarephath in the land of Sidon. And although there were many leprosy victims in Israel, Elisha healed only a foreigner, Naaman the Syrian. This kind of "unpatriotic" talk was too much for the home folks and they soon became a lynching mob.

Even Jesus' enemies were quick to see how radical this kind of talk was. On one occasion they paid him an unintended compliment by saying, "For you do not regard the position of men" [Matt. 22:16]. And they were absolutely right. In fact, our Lord decried those status seekers who, he said, liked "to go about in long robes, and to have salutations in the market places and the best seats in the synagogues and the places of honor at feasts" [Mark 12:38–39]. His criterion for a person's importance was completely different. It was, in fact, so different that even his closest followers were slow to understand and accept it.

For instance, the Gospel writer Mark tells us that one day the disciples were walking along the road arguing about, of all things, which one of them was to be greatest in the Kingdom. Later, the two brothers, James and John, went to Jesus and requested special seats of honor, one on his right hand and one on his left. Obviously, their ideas about prestige and personal status hadn't yet caught up with their Lord's. So they must have gotten a terrific jolt when Jesus said, "Whoever would be great among you must be your servant" [Mark 10:43]. For this was a completely new system in which importance was to be measured, not by the size of your bank account, but by how many persons you were serving in a helpful way.

Jesus' way of looking at people was, and still is, disturbing, because each person is seen as a child of God. It is doubtful whether any idea has ever changed the world as much as this—that the image of God is stamped eternally on each human life, and that each person, no matter how poor or ignorant, is precious in God's sight.

This, more than anything else, has completely upset the traditional grouping of people according to race, economics, or social class. It is still a constant challenge to the exploitation of the weak by the strong.

Today this idea of equality is spreading all over the world. People have been awakened to their own worth, and are demanding redress. And rightly so. No longer are the black people of this land willing to be second-class citizens, riding in the back of the bus. No longer are the hungry of the world willing to crouch quietly under the rich man's table, waiting for a few crumbs to fall. And no longer are the illiterate willing to remain locked up in the closet of intellectual darkness and be at the mercy of the elite who have obtained an education. Why such rising expectations? Because the gospel truth is out—that all people are God's children.

Sam Keen, sometimes called the "house theologian" of sensitivity training, says there are two basic revolutions taking place in our time. The one he calls the "hard revolution," which is essentially political; the other, the "soft revolution," which is personal. It is in this latter sense that the New Testament is a revolutionary document. It changes people at basic levels and gives every human being new dignity.

One time I visited a small village on the upper Nile River in Egypt, where a literacy class was meeting. One of the pupils was an old and rather feeble farmer who had walked six miles to attend the class. Afterward I asked him why he had come so far to learn to read. He spoke for many of the downtrodden of that land when he said: "This is a new day. And we have learned we are not like cattle." A revolution had taken place in the way he understood himself.

It is worth remembering that our own nation's founding fathers believed deeply in the equality of all men and wanted to establish a society where this could be demonstrated. They expressed their dream in the immortal words, "We hold these truths to be self-evident: That all men are created equal; that they are endowed by their Creator with certain unalienable rights."

Horace Mann believed deeply in this ideal and insisted that education for all was the "great equalizer." This philosophy quickly became part of the American way, and has been copied by countries all over the world. Today, our country takes great pride in the absence of royal families and the fact that anyone can "make it." Ironically, class lines have developed all the same.

Discrimination is widely practiced. I saw it recently in a New York restaurant where I went one evening for dinner. As I waited for my shish kebobs, a poorly-dressed woman in tennis shoes came in and sat at a table near enough where I could hear the conversation between her and the waiter. It was brief. The waiter walked over to her table and said, "I'm sorry, the restaurant is closed." The woman replied, "All I want is a hamburger and a cup of coffee." "Sorry, the place is closed," insisted the waiter. The poor woman reluctantly went out the door. Only a few minutes later a young fashionably dressed woman came in and sat at the same table. The same waiter greeted her with a warm smile and a large menu.

One of our great Christian journalists, the late Charles Wells, has rightly said: "Equality is still the primary issue. While at least a fourth of our population at the top live in wasteful affluence—much of it unearned—a fourth at the bottom are trapped in bleak poverty. Equality simply does not exist in this country."[14]

This being the case, the words of James should cause all of us to search our hearts. Especially in the church family, we must be certain that each person is treated as well as the next. For the royal law, "Love your neighbor as yourself," must be applied beyond the usual boundaries of economics, race, and class. At the foot of the cross the ground is very level, and no one stands higher than his brother or his sister.

CHAPTER 7

Faith at Work

"Sure, I'm a Christian, but my religion is one thing and my job is another." So says the president of First Federal Bank. "I've got problems enough," he complains, "without trying to mix my religion with how I run my business." What is this person trying to tell us? Isn't he saying that his life is lived in tightly sealed compartments, and that what happens in church on Sunday has little or nothing to do with what goes on at the bank Monday morning?

Yes, this is a strange way to live—something like playing Dr. Jekyll and Mr. Hyde. But it's a practice as old as the human race itself. It must have been common in the first century A.D., for the writer James puts it on top of the agenda for his letter to young Christians. He hits the subject head on in the first chapter, the twenty-second verse: "But be doers of the word, and not hearers only."

When James wrote these words, he was probably thinking of people he knew who attended church, listened to the Scripture-reading, and thought that had somehow made them Christians. But that's as ridiculous as walking through a university building and saying you've been through college. No, Sunday morning worship is only the beginning. From there the Christian goes out to live prayers. Surely the Lord expects this of every believer, including the bank president and all the rest of us.

In picturing the Final Judgment [Matt. 25:31–46] Jesus has

nothing to say about creeds. Instead, he made the final test a matter of what the person had done to help others in need. "I was hungry and you gave me no food, . . . sick and in prison and you did not visit me" [Matt. 25:42–43].

James likens the person who only hears the gospel and does nothing about it to a man "who observes his natural face in a mirror; for he observes himself and goes away and at once forgets what he was like" [James 1:23–24].

It was this ancient human failure that Robert Burns recognized in his familiar lines:

> Oh wad some power the giftie gie us
> To see oursels as others see us![15]

To be sure, the mirrors of James's day were different from ours—small hand pieces made of highly polished metal. But the people who held them were very much like us. A husband, ready to go out the door, is stopped in his tracks by a wife who calls: "Jacob, did you see yourself in the mirror? Your hair looks like my old mop." The already-late-for-work Jacob picks up the mirror and mumbles, "Yea, I see," and then rushes out the door completely forgetting to use his wooden comb.

Here is a striking parallel of how many people, then and now, fail to relate their religious beliefs to everyday living—the way they treat people, the way they figure their expense accounts, and the way they vote.

Surely you will agree that this is one of the most basic problems of our time. It's also one of the most serious problems in the church today. How often you hear someone say, "I might be interested in the church if there weren't so many hypocrites in it." What they usually mean is that there is too big a gap between the ideal we preach and the style of life we live. Just the other day a man asked, "Is so-and-so a Christian?" I said I thought so, and he replied: "I don't see how he can be. He worries too much." There's the gap. Mahatma Gandhi used to say that Christians were just ordinary people who made extraordinary claims. And James was troubled by the same credibility gap—people who just talked the faith, but didn't live it.

In addition, James had an even more serious problem. There were people in the early church who were saying flatly that it didn't make any difference—that you could live any way you wanted so long as you had your name on the roll and professed to have faith. The tone and length of James's argument show that he regarded this as spiritual suicide. He asks:

> What does it profit, my brethren, if a man says he has faith but has not works? Can his faith save him? If a brother or sister is ill-clad and in lack of daily food, and one of you says to them, "Go in peace, be warmed and filled," without giving them the things needed for the body, what does it profit? So faith by itself, if it has no works, is dead. [James 2:14–17]

Here we are confronted with the central point of The Epistle of James—that good works are an essential part of the Christian's life. We say, "Fair enough," but it is this very point of the book which is most often criticized. The critics mistakenly assume that James is here contradicting the apostle Paul, who said that justification is by faith alone. But on more careful reading, it becomes clear that James does nothing of the kind. The Christians to whom he wrote were probably followers of Paul. But if so, they had misunderstood what the apostle meant when he used the word "faith." They thought "faith" was simply an intellectual belief like saying, "God is One." James shocks them by writing that even the demons can say such things.

The truth of the matter is that even for Paul faith was never just intellectual belief. To the contrary, it was a matter of giving oneself over to a new way of life, something Paul called "life in Christ." He taught that belief in Christ was the first step in becoming a Christian, but it was never the end.

And to his dying day he fought those who assumed that it was. In Rom. 6:1 he writes: "What shall we say then? Are we to continue in sin that grace may abound? By no means!"

So it is clear that while Paul insisted that salvation could not be earned by works, he always assumed that the works of one's daily life were the final test of faith. Many parts of his letters include a kind of checklist of the sort of behavior that constitutes a truly Christian life-style. For instance, in his letter to the Ephesians he writes: "I therefore . . . beg you to lead a life worthy of the calling to which you have been called" [Eph. 4:1]. Then he spends the second half of the book dealing with the practical matter of living the Christian life out in the world. He says, "Therefore, putting away falsehood, let everyone speak the truth with his neighbor. . . . Let the thief no longer steal. . . . Let no evil talk come out of your mouths" [Eph. 4:25–29]. Remember, also, it was Paul who wrote: "If I have all faith, so as to remove mountains, but have not love, I am nothing" [I Cor. 13:2].

So, what appears at first to be a contradiction between James and Paul turns out to be simply two ways of saying the same thing—that Christian faith must result in practical down-to-earth goodness. In this, the Bible stands firm, a direct challenge to anybody today who is content to say certain words, like "amen" and "hallelujah," but who are not prepared to apply their faith to the business of everyday living, including the practical needs of people in their community.

This is still one of the big issues facing the local church. For many congregations today are still polarized between faith and works. Half the members think the church should concentrate its efforts on so-called "spiritual" things such as prayer, Bible study, and evangelism, while the other half want to challenge city hall on its zoning policy, collect food for a hunger center, or build a group home for underprivileged young people.

From the book of James we learn that either emphasis,

without the other, is only half the gospel, and that in the matter of faith and works, as in the traditional marriage ceremony, we need the reminder, "What God has joined together, let no man put asunder."

William Barclay sums it up succinctly: "No man will ever be moved to action without faith; and no man's faith is real until it moves him to action."[16]

Where in your life can you do a better job of relating your faith in your actions?

THE LETTER
OF
JAMES

Let not many of you become teachers, my brethren, for you know that we who teach shall be judged with greater strictness. ²For we all make many mistakes, and if any one makes no mistakes in what he says he is a perfect man, able to bridle the whole body also. ³If we put bits into the mouths of horses that they may obey us, we guide their whole bodies. ⁴Look at the ships also; though they are so great and are driven by strong winds, they are guided by a very small rudder wherever the will of the pilot directs. ⁵So the tongue is a little member and boasts of great things. How great a forest is set ablaze by a small fire!

6 And the tongue is a fire. The tongue is an unrighteous world among our members, staining the whole body, setting on fire the cycle of nature,[b] and set on fire by hell[c] ⁷For every kind of beast and bird, of reptile and sea creature, can be tamed and has been tamed by humankind, ⁸but no human being can tame the tongue—a restless evil, full of deadly poison. ⁹With it we bless the Lord and Father, and with it we curse men, who are made in the likeness of God. ¹⁰From the

[b] Or *wheel of birth*
[c] Greek *Gehenna*

same mouth come blessing and cursing. My brethren, this ought not to be so. [11]Does a spring pour forth from the same opening fresh water and brackish? [12]Can a fig tree, my brethren, yield olives, or a grapevine figs? No more can salt water yield fresh.

13 Who is wise and understanding among you? By his good life let him show his works in the meekness of wisdom. [14]But if you have bitter jealousy and selfish ambition in your hearts, do not boast and be false to the truth. [15]This wisdom is not such as comes down from above, but is earthly, unspiritual, devilish. [16]For where jealousy and selfish ambition exist, there will be disorder and every vile practice. [17]But the wisdom from above is first pure, then peaceable, gentle, open to reason, full of mercy and good fruits, without uncertainty or insincerity. [18]And the harvest of righteousness is sown in peace by those who make peace.

CHAPTER 8

The Gift of Wisdom

To endure hardship, and benefit from it, requires a great deal of wisdom. So James writes: "If any of you lacks wisdom, let him ask God . . ." [James 1:5]. We noted earlier that the book of James is similar in style to Proverbs: here we come to common subject matter. Today, many of us think of wisdom as cleverness or the ability to get by in a highly competitive society. But for James, wisdom is the ability to see beyond surface appearances and to know what is right and wrong. In this sense James follows the Biblical writers before him who always spoke of wisdom as a moral and religious quality. For instance, the "wisdom of Solomon" is celebrated in legend and the Bible, but even Solomon understood it to be a spiritual gift. As his rule began, Solomon prayed for an "understanding mind . . . [to] discern between good and evil" [I Kings 3:9]. It was no human achievement, but the gift of God. The Scripture is clear. "God gave Solomon wisdom and understanding beyond measure" [I Kings 4:29].

Modern man would do well to seek this same divine gift. The crisis of our age is that knowledge has advanced faster than wisdom. For example, our scientists and technologists know how to harness energy from nuclear fusion, but our very survival is threatened because they are unclear as to how this knowledge should be used. At first, we were assured that each nuclear nation would never be the first to drop a nuclear bomb. Now it is frightening to learn that there is no such commitment and that each is ready to use nuclear force at its own discretion for the sake of what is called "national interest." Our own Government has made it clear that nuclear force is not ruled out in any struggle where our vital interests seem threatened. This situation caused Arnold Toynbee to observe that "technical proficiency is not, in itself, a guarantee of wisdom and survival."[17] Here the great British historian is saying in modern terms what the Bible has been saying for three thousand years: that wisdom is more than knowledge and technical know-how. In the third chapter of his letter, James spells it out in more detail.

> Who is wise and understanding among you? By his good life let him show his works in the meekness of wisdom. But if you have bitter jealousy and selfish ambition in your hearts, do not boast and be false to the truth. This wisdom is not such as comes down from above, but is earthly, unspiritual, devilish. For where jealousy and selfish ambition exist, there will be disorder and every vile practice. [James 3:13–16]

Apparently there were some of James's readers who thought they were wise but who gave no evidence of it in their everyday life-style. Instead, they were ill-mannered, undisciplined, jealous, and driven by self-centered ambition. James says that true wisdom must result in a good life, just as faith must be accompanied by works. Any claim to wisdom that does not result in good conduct is false and as empty as a balloon on a string.

Today our American way of life is so achievement- and competition-oriented that wisdom is easily equated with cleverness and the ability to "succeed." In politics this led some to believe that even "dirty tricks" were permissible as long as they were used for a good cause (their cause) and as long as they could be covered up. By now we know, however, that such deceitful behavior ultimately destroys the person who practices it, whether he be a sixth-grade schoolboy or president of the United States. Equally clear is the fact that it destroys the community.

James tells us that where such things are practiced, there will be disorder of every kind. This false wisdom, says James, is clearly not "from above," but is earthly. It is the same distinction the apostle Paul makes in his first letter to the Corinthians. He writes: "Has not God made foolish the wisdom of the world?" [I Cor. 1:20]. He then goes on to write of a "wisdom of God" which everyone should seek.

James tells us that the wisdom from God is first of all "pure." For some, this word "pure" may suggest sexual virtue. Surely that is part of wisdom, but here the word means something different. It means being straightforward in our relationships with others, with no hidden agenda, with no ulterior motive. It is just opposite to the way some people operate. They are so devious that you begin to wonder what they are up to when they act kindly or say something nice. But think how your own family would be strengthened, how your work relations would improve if each person could always be honest without trying to manipulate the other. That's one of the ingredients of true wisdom.

Another is peace and harmony. Today few things seem harder to achieve. Ours is a confused and splintered world in which we seem powerless against the centrifugal forces pulling us apart from one another. Perhaps we've lived too long under the illusion that it's easy to build community. For instance, in race relations we thought that if we just passed a few laws and brought people close to one another, the job would be done. But experience has taught us some hard lessons. Now we know that to bring people close together may mean merely an increased knowledge of each other's faults and an intolerable clashing of self-interest.

The continuing rise in the divorce rate is further evidence of the divisive forces at work. And perhaps the most tragic reminder of all is the frequency of quarrels within some Christian churches. Peace and harmony seem to be ever just beyond our reach. More wisdom will help because it is peaceable.

Wisdom is also meek. This word isn't used much anymore, but it is still important. Jesus said, "Blessed are the meek, for they shall inherit the earth." Probably this Beatitude has been ridiculed more than any other, because a meek person is thought to be mousy and weak.

This understanding is unfortunate, because originally the word "meek" was applied to animals that were tamed and domesticated. The term never implied weakness. For instance, the Burma elephant that goes crashing wildly through the jungle and then is trained to pile teak logs is not made weaker by the training. His energies simply have been brought under control. Likewise, the harnessed donkey in James's day was called meek—not because it was weak but because its strength was being put to use. Similarly, Christian meekness means that a person has given his energies to Christ. In this way his spiritual strength has more direction and purpose. Because he is meek, the Christian is stronger and more useful.

Next, James tells us that wisdom is "open to reason." Can you think of anything more needed today? Families are polarized, communities have lost their unity because so many people have made absolutes out of their own opinions. For example, it is common to hear people say of their own point of view, "It isn't even open for discussion." Now, the real tragedy is not that people have so many different opinions, but that so many have sealed off any real communication. Each person has become an island. In contrast, the Christian with wisdom is at all times open to reason, amenable, ready to listen, and always conciliatory.

What's more, James says, "wisdom is full of mercy." It is compassionate to those in trouble or need. Here again he is close to the teaching of our Lord, who said: "Go and learn what this means, 'I desire mercy, and not sacrifice' " [Matt. 9:13; 12:7]. It reminds us of the prophet Micah, who denounced the outward religiosity of his people and said, "He has showed you, O man, what is good; and what does the LORD require of you but to do justice, and to love kindness, and to walk humbly with your God?" [Micah 6:8]. Why is it that so many Christians find it easier to insist on justice than to practice mercy? The morally upright person can be intensely cruel, lacking in human kindness. Here again, more wisdom would help.

Our writer goes on to tell us that wisdom is "full of good fruit." This is picture language referring to deeds of practical goodness. It takes us back to the first thing James said about wisdom, namely, that it must result in positive goodness.

Finally, James tells us that wisdom is "without uncertainty," meaning without partiality and favoritism. It is also "without insincerity." In other words, there is no pretense, affectation, or double-dealing. Persons with Christian wisdom are instead always open and honest in all their relationships. They are even-handed in dealing with their children. They take the word of the apostle Paul seriously, "Let love be genuine" [Rom. 12:9].

Reviewing James's description of true wisdom, we can't help wondering about its breadth. It is nothing less than Christlike living. Why not rate yourself on a scale from one to five on the marks of true wisdom? Where are you strong? And where are you weak? Remember, wisdom is pure, peaceful, meek, open to reason, full of mercy, without affectation, and it is evidenced in practical everyday goodness.

We ask, "Who is sufficient to these things?" In this sense, who can be wise? James answers clearly—anyone who sincerely wants to be. This takes us back where we started: "If any of you lacks wisdom, let him ask God . . ." [James 1:5]. And why ask God? Because wisdom is nothing we can manufacture. We cannot attain it by our own effort. It is a gift.

It can be yours for the asking, but you must ask in faith. It means coming to God in confidence that he hears and will give what you ask. Here we need to believe the promise of our Lord, "Ask, . . . and you will receive" [Matt. 21:22].

CHAPTER 9

The Mightiest Muscle

Some serious problems must have been caused in the early church by members who had not yet learned to discipline their tongues. Otherwise, why would James have brought up the subject four times in this brief epistle? He introduces the matter first in ch. 1:10: "Let every man be quick to hear and slow to speak." This illustrates the terse style of the book, but also reminds us of particular verses in Proverbs which James himself may have had in mind. For instance:

> He who guards his mouth preserves his life;
>   he who opens wide his lips comes to ruin.
> [Prov. 13:3]

Later we find the writer laughing to himself:

> Even a fool who keeps silent is considered wise;
>   when he closes his lips, he is deemed intelligent.
> [Prov. 17:28]

The injunction of James to be sparing in one's words may have been directed to Christian zealots who used strong and angry language against their Roman rulers. Or, more likely, it was intended for some new Christians who were overly anxious to impress their views on others, and were becoming angry when people didn't agree with them.

Furthermore, from the third chapter it is clear that some persons in the early church were eager to teach, but were not qualified. James doesn't tell us how one becomes qualified, but rather stresses the serious moral responsibility one assumes who desires to speak as a teacher. Even today some people look at the vocation of the teacher or the preacher and see only the dubious prestige connected with it. James is saying, Look beyond the prestige and be sure you understand the serious obligation involved.

On the other hand, James may have had in mind particular persons who prayed in pious tones at the love feast and afterward cussed out their brothers in foul language.

> But no human being can tame the tongue. . . . With it we bless the Lord and Father, and with it we curse men, who are made in the likeness of God. From the same mouth come blessing and cursing. My brethren, this ought not to be so. [James 3:8–12]

He then goes on to argue from nature for consistency either for the good use or the bad use of the tongue.

Christians are called to be so consistent in the language they use that their identity will always be clear to everyone. This involves not merely avoiding the commonly used four-letter words, but more importantly, guarding the manner in which one talks to the person who has been insulting. For how can one bless God in one breath and curse his children in the next? A mountain spring always gives fresh water, not fresh one day and brackish the next.

Now we come to look at the tongue more closely. James singles it out as the mightiest muscle of the human body. He first likens it to the bit the farmer puts in the horse's mouth —small but able to turn the powerful animal in any direction. Next he compares it to the rudder of a ship—almost insignificant in size but able to take the sailing vessel wherever the captain wants it to go. Finally, he compares the tongue to a spark that sets off a terrible forest fire.

These three analogies are strikingly different, but all make the same point: the human tongue is important all out of proportion to its size. While it is one of the smallest members of the body, it is one of the most powerful.

Many of us would feel more comfortable with these comparisons if they ended on a positive note showing how much good the tongue can do. But the writer was so concerned to correct those who were undisciplined in their speech that he talks only of the potential dangers.

Finally, James brings the whole discussion down to the level of interpersonal relations and the importance of maintaining a strong bond of fellowship in the church. In ch. 4:11 he writes: "Do not speak evil against one another, brethren." The reference here is to the common practice of slandering someone behind the person's back. This is condemned all through the Bible. For instance, the psalmist reports God as saying, "Him who slanders his neighbor secretly, I will destroy" [Ps. 101:5]. The apostle Paul calls it "backbiting," and lists it among the sins of pagans. James condemns it on two counts. First, the law of Christ says we should love our neighbor as ourself. And speaking evil of another person is clearly a violation of this law of love. The other reason slander is wrong is that it violates our Lord's command, "Judge not." If we pass judgment on another person, we have assumed the prerogative of God.

Here is a sin clearly condemned by Jesus in the Sermon on the Mount, denounced by Paul in his letter to Romans, and now laid bare by The Epistle of James. Still it creeps back into the life of many churches today. In fact, it is often the religious and morally upright person who is most judgmental. We see it in the parable that Jesus gave of the Pharisee and the publican at prayer. We see it too in the attitude of church members today toward those who have done wrong, particularly those of public prominence.

The fact is that the inclination to judge others is never far from any of us. It must be somehow related to the need to fortify our own sense of worth. And this is part of the very reason it is wrong. For it is sinful to tear down our neighbor in order to build ourselves up:

> Why, I wonder, do we think
> Approval we can win,
> By spreading the statistics
> Of other people's sins?[18]

How badly all of us need to relearn how to use our tongue for positive things such as building others up and sharing insights rather than for petty criticism and put-downs.

A poem by Beth Day about 150 years ago fits this emphasis of James very well.

> . . . Make it pass,
> Before you speak, three gates of gold:
> These narrow gates. First, "Is it true?"
> Then, "Is it needful?" In your mind
> Give truthful answer. And the next
> Is last and narrowest, "Is it kind?"
> And if to reach your lips at last
> It passes through these gates three,
> Then you may tell the tale, nor fear.
> What the result of speech may be.[19]

You can be sure that every word you speak leaves a mark on someone. It can be a painful thing. Or it can be a word of healing. Many people ask, "How can I do anything for Christ today?" One way to begin is to be more careful about your speech, the way you use your tongue. Consider the people you are going to see tomorrow. Write down their names and one thing you like about them. Then ask the Lord to help you say something tomorrow that will bring out your good feelings and affirm the best in those you meet.

THE LETTER OF

JAMES

What causes wars, and what causes fightings among you? Is it not your passions that are at war in your members? ²You desire and do not have; so you kill. And you covet[d] and cannot obtain; so you fight and wage war. You do not have, because you do not ask. ³You ask and do not receive, because you ask wrongly, to spend it on your passions. ⁴Unfaithful creatures! Do you not know that friendship with the world is enmity with God? Therefore whoever wishes to be a friend of the world makes himself an enemy of God. ⁵Or do you suppose it is in vain that the scripture says, "He yearns jealously over the spirit which he has made to dwell in us"? ⁶But he gives more grace; therefore it says, "God opposes the proud, but gives grace to the humble." ⁷Submit yourselves therefore to God. Resist the devil and he will flee from you. ⁸Draw near to God and he will draw near to you. Cleanse your hands, you sinners, and purify your hearts, you men of double mind. ⁹Be wretched and mourn and weep. Let your laughter be turned to mourning and your joy to dejection. ¹⁰Humble yourselves before the Lord and he will exalt you.

4

[d] Or *you kill and you covet*

11 Do not speak evil against one another, brethren. He that speaks evil against a brother or judges his brother, speaks evil against the law and judges the law. But if you judge the law, you are not a doer of the law but a judge. [12]There is one lawgiver and judge, he who is able to save and to destroy. But who are you that you judge your neighbor?

13 Come now, you who say, "Today or tomorrow we will go into such and such a town and spend a year there and trade and get gain"; [14]whereas you do not know about tomorrow. What is your life? For you are a mist that appears for a little time and then vanishes. [15]Instead you ought to say, "If the Lord wills, we shall live and we shall do this or that." [16]As it is, you boast in your arrogance. All such boasting is evil. [17]Whoever knows what is right to do and fails to do it, for him it is sin.

CHAPTER 10

God Willing

Human arrogance is one of the most prevalent, yet least understood, sins of our time. And we're all guilty. What kind of plans are you making for the future? A trip to Florida? Enclosing the porch? Finding ten new accounts? Or just spending more time with the family? In all of this, is there anywhere in your thoughts a clear recognition that your times are in God's hands?

This is important, for it is always tempting to make our plans for the future as if God didn't exist. The New Testament writer James tells us with strong feeling that to live this way is a sin. He points his finger at a typical businessman, and writes:

> Come now, you who say, "Today or tomorrow we will go into such and such a town and spend a year there and trade and get gain"; whereas you do not know about tomorrow. What is your life? For you are a mist that appears for a little time and then vanishes. Instead you ought to say, "If the Lord wills, we shall live and we shall do this or that." As it is, you boast in your arrogance. All such boasting is evil. [James 4:13–16]

The picture was a familiar one to James's first readers. They could visualize a merchant packing his chariot for a trip to the big city, where he would buy and sell in the hope of making a good profit. It's interesting that James doesn't condemn the man for speculating or for profit making. Rather, he assumes such activity to be normal. What he finds completely unchristian is making such plans without any recognition of, or any dependence on, God. Underneath the man's planning was human arrogance, evidenced in his doing business as if he were completely self-sufficient.

Americans may have more difficulty with this sin than do people of some other cultures. For all of us have been taught from childhood that one of the characteristic American virtues is self-reliance. We were told that independence was the quality that brought the Pilgrims over here in the first place and that later opened up the western frontiers. Then, growing up, many of us admired Horatio Alger, a fictional self-sufficient man whose persistence and resourcefulness always brought success. We were convinced we could be like him if we wanted to be.

An uncle of mine was fiercely independent and proud. As a boy I always admired him when he boasted, "There isn't anything I can't do if you give me enough time." But in his arrogance he cut himself off from his spiritual roots and from his own family. Finally the walls of his emotional strength came tumbling down as if hit by a battering ram. A grim reminder that none of us can go it alone. We are made by God, and we are dependent on him. To assume otherwise is to invite spiritual disaster.

All of us will do well to reread the works of Reinhold Niebuhr, who taught us to see that human pride is the raw material out of which all sin is made. In his book *Beyond Tragedy,* Niebuhr wrote:

> Man always remains a creature and his sin arises from the fact that he is not satisfied to remain so. He seeks to turn creatureliness into infinity; whereas his salvation depends upon subjecting his creaturely weakness to the infinite good of God.[20]

This sin of arrogance easily takes root in a secular culture like ours, but modern man didn't invent it. It is as old as the human race. It was the basic flaw of the first pair, Adam and Eve. You'll remember, God told them not to eat of the tree of knowledge. On the other hand, the serpent tempted them with the promise: "You will be like God" [Gen. 3:5]. So their real temptation was not their hunger for fresh fruit. It was, rather, to defy their God-given limitations.

We have special problems along the same lines today. We live in a garden of technology, and for many, "scientism" has become a new faith. For instance, the first moon landing, in April 1967, gave some people an almost ultimate kind of confidence in man—the belief that scientific man can do anything. It isn't that we human beings now profess to know everything. But we do believe we can know everything if just given enough time. Here again, Niebuhr warns us: "The achievements of science and technics have beguiled us into a false complacency. We have forgotten the frailty of man."[21] It is precisely for this reason that we find it hard to follow James's advice, to condition our plans with the words "God willing."

In contrast, many of our forefathers took James literally. They even added the initials D.V. to their documents and personal papers. The initials were the first letters of the Latin words *Deo volente,* which means "God willing." Muslims of the Arab world often use the term *Inshallah,* which means the same thing. Growing up in a Mennonite family, I remember my father often saying to friends, "I'll be over at your place on such and such a day, God willing."

This kind of thinking comes hard for us today, for we have developed an exaggerated idea of our ability to run the world alone. Humility now heads the list of modern shortages.

The truth is that our illusion of self-sufficiency has swollen to dangerous proportions. We have become immodest about our place in the universe and our relation to the environment. New judgment waits at the door in terms of critical energy shortages and even the destruction of the protective ozone layer. Furthermore, we have sacrificed human values for economic growth and power. We have put material things in our life where God belongs—our job, security, gadgets, prestige, and power.

What is true on the personal level is also true of society at large. The pretensions of human culture and nationalism are simple reflections of this same basic pride. But to forget the finiteness of our social and political systems, even time-honored democracy, is to substitute human institutions for God. We must never forget that we are mortal, and so is our culture.

This is one of the lessons, if not the central one, in the Genesis story about the Tower of Babel. Some may wish to regard the story as simply a primitive explanation of how we came to have so many languages. But it is a mistake to miss human sin and God's judgment in the story. You see, God's dwelling was thought to be in the heavens. So men said, "Come, let us build ourselves a city, and a tower with its top in the heavens, and let us make a name for ourselves."

While that may be primitive, it is still a profound reminder of humanity's besetting sin of self-will and pride. The Tower of Babel was literally only seven stories high, but its real purpose was to transcend man's finite limitations. For this reason God confused the builders so they couldn't even communicate with one another, and they had to call off the whole project.

Mankind today doesn't compete with God in so crass and primitive a fashion, but just as surely we deny our nature and proclaim in arrogance: "Anything God can do, we can do better." And just as surely, divine judgment is upon us. For how else can one explain the confusion of our times? Our divisions are just as tragic and even more widespread than those of Babel.

James was close to the teachings and example of his Lord

when he told us to condition our plans with the phrase "God willing." In the Beatitudes, Jesus put humility first. "Blessed are the poor in spirit," he said, "for theirs is the kingdom of heaven" [Matt. 5:3]. Furthermore, many of his parables exalted the same virtue. In one of them, the self-righteous Pharisee said, "God, I thank thee that I am not like other men" [Luke 18:11]. And the despised tax collector didn't as much as dare lift his eyes up to heaven. But note that it was the humble man and not the arrogant one who went to his house justified that day. In another parable, a wealthy farmer decided that he would tear down his barns and build bigger ones. His folly became apparent when he died suddenly and his soul was required of him.

In sharpest contrast, Jesus took the will of God into account at every turn of his own life. John reports our Lord saying, "I seek not my own will but the will of him who sent me" [John 5:30]. And again, "He who sent me is with me; he has not left me alone, for I always do what is pleasing to him" [John 8:29].

It is in the example of our Lord that James's instruction to say "If God wills" reaches its highest fulfillment.

Will you follow his example as you plan for tomorrow? Remember James's advice (paraphrased): "Come on, you who say, 'I've got some big plans!' Don't be presumptuous. You may not even be here tomorrow." What you ought to be saying is, "If the Lord wills, and I'm still around, I'll do this or that in the days ahead."

CHAPTER 11

"Judge Not"

Have you ever wondered why the New Testament tells us so emphatically not to judge other people? In the Sermon on the Mount, Jesus said, "Judge not, that you be not judged" [Matt. 7:1]. Then, in his letter to the Romans, Paul wrote, "Therefore you have no excuse, O man, whoever you are, when you judge another" [Rom. 2:1]. And finally, in The Epistle of James, we read, "Who are you that you judge your neighbor?" [James 4:12].

Why these strictures against judging others? Is it possible for any of us to go through life without passing judgment on other people? Aren't we expected to evaluate character as accurately as possible? Certainly these Biblical prohibitions against judging cannot mean that we should be blind to the moral failures of our age.

Furthermore, didn't Jesus himself tell us: "The tree is known by its fruit," and even more sharply, "Do not throw your pearls before swine"? No New Testament writer puts more emphasis on discriminating morality than James. He condemns those who do not practice what they preach and who are too free with their tongue, and he addresses the wayward unmistakenly as "You sinners." Isn't that judging? All of this forces us to conclude that the command "Judge not" was never intended to discourage moral appraisal which is so essential to human relations. Rather, it must refer to the hypocritical condemnation of other people done in a

76

spirit of superiority. Such criticism is destructive, with no concern for the other person's welfare. One of my old seminary professors used to say of the judgment here proscribed: "It is judgment without knowledge, without love, and without necessity."

Apparently there was enough of this judgment in the early church to cause James deep concern. He writes in chapter 4, verse 11:

> Do not speak evil against one another, brethren. He that speaks evil against a brother or judges his brother, speaks evil against the law and judges the law.

Again, in chapter 5, verse 9, he writes:

> Do not grumble, brethren, against one another, that you may not be judged; behold, the Judge is standing at the doors.

From these verses it appears that when the Bible tells us not to judge others, it is talking about careless criticism and slander, especially in the church. With that clarification, we are now ready to ask "Why?" Why should we avoid judging one another? Well, the first and most obvious reason is that we are so often wrong. None of us is omniscient, so we judge only by appearances. By now we should know that appearances can be misleading. Take, for instance, the matter of long hair on men. I don't happen to like it. But I have had to stop judging all men with long hair as antiestablishment types because I have found underneath a lot of hair some of the most sensitive and public-spirited people I know. It's only a reminder that we usually judge by appearances, and that we can easily be wrong. That's probably why the Jews even before Jesus' time had a saying in their Mishnah, "Do not judge your fellow until you are in his position." It reminds me of an American Indian saying: "Do not criticize another until you have walked in his moccasins for two weeks."

A second reason we should refrain from judging other people is that such judging destroys community. The bonds of fellowship are quickly broken when persons are censorious and critical of one another. This can spell disaster for the home in which the husband and wife are always placing blame on each other. And it can tear a church apart no matter how strong it has been in the past.

The pity of it is that such criticism is highly contagious. Perhaps it grows out of self-defense. If my family is criticized, I'm likely to look for something to criticize in the critic. And if someone finds fault with my appearance, I'm going to look for faults in that person. Since no one is perfect, there is always fault to be found. And so the process goes on in endless circles until the tie that binds is reduced to a thin thread.

A third reason we should avoid judging others is that criticism by us of someone else is often a reflection on ourselves. The words of Jesus, "Judge not, that you be not judged" are a clear reminder. When we criticize others we reveal ourselves. For instance, if we call someone else "nosy," we are confessing that we are familiar with the symptoms and may in reality be criticizing one of our own pet sins.

I had an uncle who was constantly criticizing people whom he called "tightwads." But he would never take a newspaper because it was "too expensive." I had another who was forever calling other people lazy. And when we would go camping together he would lie under the shade tree and tell us boys how to put up his tent.

This business of judging others is something like looking at a great painting. In our criticism of the painting the picture is really judging us.

Jesus likened it to a man who pointed out a small speck in his friend's eye while never mentioning the fact that he had a huge log in his own.

The great English writer John Donne said, "Jesus never

laughed." But I don't believe it. Surely he must have laughed when he said, "Why do you see the speck that is in your brother's eye, but do not notice the log that is in your own eye?" [Matt. 7:3].

Still another reason we should be done with judging others is that life pretty much gives back what we put into it. If we pour in slander, the poison is likely to appear on our own table. Again, Jesus gave us clear warning when he said, "The measure you give will be the measure you get" [Matt. 7:2]. And his words, "All who take the sword will perish by the sword" [Matt. 26:52] have applications far beyond the battlefield. Haven't you observed that the person who is cruel in his talk about other people often becomes the victim of adverse public opinion? Contaminate the well, and you're likely to drink contaminated water.

But the most important word on judging has yet to be said. The real reason we are not to judge others is that that's not our job. Judgment belongs finally to God—not to man. The Bible is clear: "Vengeance is mine, I will repay, says the Lord" [Rom. 12:19].

When any of us judges our fellowman we are in effect asking God to move over so we can sit on his throne. How ridiculous! We see only the window dressing. He looks at the heart.

Furthermore, all of us are under the same judgment of God. As we stand before his righteousness, who dares condemn another? It is only by God's love and forgiveness that any of us dare stand. He expects us to be loving and long on forgiveness in dealing with the faults of others. In this matter Jesus is not only our teacher but our example par excellence. Remember his words on the cross. As he hung there dying, we hear no haranguing or condemning the soldiers, but rather the prayer, "Father, forgive them; for they know not what they do" [Luke 23:34]. It was this spirit the writer James wanted to see in the church. His words do not go out of date:

Do not speak evil against one another, brethren. He that speaks evil against a brother . . . speaks evil against the law and judges the law. But if you judge the law, you are not a doer of the law but a judge. There is one lawgiver and judge, he who is able to save and to destroy. But who are you that you judge your neighbor? [James 4:11–12]

If anybody asks you tomorrow what the Bible says about judging, you may answer simply, "Cut it out!"

CHAPTER 12

The Sin of Doing Nothing

When a person does nothing and is pronounced guilty, that's news. But according to the Bible, it happens all the time. James writes: "Whoever knows what is right to do and fails to do it, for him it is sin" [James 4:17].

This is a real switch from our usual way of thinking. We've been taught that Adam and Eve sinned when they ate the forbidden fruit. Cain sinned when, in a fit of jealousy, he killed his brother, Abel. Someone holds up the First National Bank or cheats on his income tax. We have no difficulty identifying these actions as sins. But such usual cataloging can mislead us because it leaves out the chief sin of most of us—the sin of doing nothing.

James's word on this subject is another of those "pearls" we talked about in the first chapter. It stands by itself, unrelated to anything that precedes or follows. Indeed, it may have been a common saying of James's day which he included for its own intrinsic worth. To some, it may look like a general moralism, completely lacking any Christian character. But closer examination puts it alongside the Golden Rule and other teachings of Jesus for its emphasis on positive goodness. The rabbis had long known the Golden Rule in negative terms. "Don't do anything to your neighbor that you wouldn't like him to do to you." It was Jesus who turned this around and said: "Whatever you wish that men would do to you, do so to them" [Matt. 7:12].

James was simply stating a corollary to these well-known words of our Lord that a person who knows what he should do and refuses is committing a sin.

The church needs periodically to hear these words. For Christianity must never be reduced to a set of negatives, no matter how important some of the "Thou shalt nots" may be. Christian faith and discipleship is rather a positive call to be something and to do something. And today we need James's reminder that there is another kind of sin besides transgression of the moral law. It is the sin of inaction when action is needed.

This is why many churches use the familiar prayer of confession which says, "We have done those things we ought not to have done and we have left undone those things we ought to have done." This latter kind of sin—the sin of omission—comes into sharp focus in a number of Jesus' parables. Take, for instance, the one we call the good Samaritan [Luke 10:29–37]. The story almost takes for granted that there will always be violent persons such as robbers around. But the most scathing condemnation is left for the people who did nothing. The very persons who should have cared most—the religious leaders—passed by on the other side of the road. If there had been an investigation of the crime, all of them could have said, quite rightly, "We didn't do anything." And that is just the point of the story.

Or take the parable of the rich man and Lazarus [Luke 16:19–31]. It is notable that the rich man is not condemned for being wealthy or for cheating his neighbor or for beating his wife. He is condemned for doing nothing. Day after day he saw Lazarus, clad in the poorest rags, underfed and slowly dying of starvation. He let the poor man have a few scraps from his table, but did nothing to change the situation.

Today there is a long list of unfinished business on the

Christian agenda, but too many church people are ready to turn the page with the excuse, "We've done all we can do." But our Lord asks: "If you've done all you can do about world hunger, then why will millions of men, women, and children starve this year? And if you've done all you can do on the race issue, then why are your neighborhoods still segregated and school busing the last resort? If you've done what is needful for ecology, then why are the dead fish being washed up on the shores of Lake Erie?"

You see, we have left undone those things we should have done. Indifference to human need is surely one area where the warning of James is most applicable. It is caused partly by what Norman Cousins calls "compassion fatigue." We see so much human suffering on our television screens and read so much about it in our papers that we tend to become calloused. Or we rationalize. As a schoolteacher said recently: "None of us can care about everybody. The world is just too big. So we have to pull down the blinds on some of it."

Granted, we all have our limitations, in terms of material resources, technical competence, and emotional strength. But it is still true, as George Bernard Shaw once wrote, that "the worst sin toward our fellow creatures is not to hate them, but to be indifferent to them."[22]

This indifference was the whole point of our Lord's disturbing picture of the Last Judgment, recorded in Matt., ch. 25. The shocking thing about this picture is that many people who thought they were good stood condemned before the bar of divine justice. They had not murdered, stolen, or committed adultery. Rather, in the face of human need they had simply failed to show kindness. Specifically, they had not visited the sick, the imprisoned, the offcasts of society. They had not offered a cup of cold water to the neighbor who was thirsty. They had done nothing. And that's what condemned them. It was that which caused the King to say, "Depart from me."

Let us pray each day for God to show us what he wants us to do, and grant us courage to do it, so that someday we may hear the King say, "Well done, good and faithful servant; . . . enter into the joy of your master" [Matt. 25:21].

THE LETTER
OF
JAMES

Come now, you rich, weep and howl for the miseries that are coming upon you. [2]Your riches have rotted and your garments are moth-eaten. [3]Your gold and silver have rusted, and their rust will be evidence against you and will eat your flesh like fire. You have laid up treasure[e] for the last days. [4]Behold, the wages of the laborers who mowed your fields, which you kept back by fraud, cry out; and the cries of the harvesters have reached the ears of the Lord of hosts. [5]You have lived on the earth in luxury and in pleasure; you have fattened your hearts in a day of slaughter. [6]You have condemned, you have killed the righteous man; he does not resist you.

7 Be patient, therefore, brethren, until the coming of the Lord. Behold, the farmer waits for the precious fruit of the earth, being patient over it until it receives the early and the late rain. [8]You also be patient. Establish your hearts, for the coming of the Lord is at hand. [9]Do not grumble, brethren, against one another, that you may not be judged; behold, the Judge is standing at the doors. [10]As an example of suffering and patience, brethren, take the prophets who spoke in the name of

[e] Or *will eat your flesh, since you have stored up fire*

the Lord. [11]Behold, we call those happy who were steadfast. You have heard of the steadfastness of Job, and you have seen the purpose of the Lord, how the Lord is compassionate and merciful.

12 But above all, my brethren, do not swear, either by heaven or by earth or with any other oath, but let your yes be yes and your no be no, that you may not fall under condemnation.

13 Is any one among you suffering? Let him pray. Is any cheerful? Let him sing praise. [14]Is any among you sick? Let him call for the elders of the church, and let them pray over him, anointing him with oil in the name of the Lord; [15]and the prayer of faith will save the sick man, and the Lord will raise him up; and if he has committed sins, he will be forgiven. [16]Therefore confess your sins to one another, and pray for one another, that you may be healed. The prayer of a righteous man has great power in its effects. [17]Eli'jah was a man of like nature with ourselves and he prayed fervently that it might not rain, and for three years and six months it did not rain on the earth. [18]Then he prayed again and the heaven gave rain, and the earth brought forth its fruit.

19 My brethren, if any one among you wanders from the truth and some one brings him back, [20]let him know that whoever brings back a sinner from the error of his way will save his soul from death and will cover a multitude of sins.

CHAPTER 13

Tainted Profits

It is sometimes said that the church should stick to the Bible and stay out of politics and economics. But the Bible itself doesn't stay out of these things. In fact, as William Barclay has well said: "There is no book in any literature with such a burning social passion as the Bible."[23]

This being the case, it shouldn't surprise us too much to find some pretty strong words about business ethics in The Epistle of James. In the fifth chapter we read:

Come now, you rich, weep and howl for the miseries that are coming upon you. Your riches have rotted and your garments are moth-eaten. Your gold and silver have rusted, and their rust will be evidence against you and will eat your flesh like fire. You have laid up treasure for the last days. Behold, the wages of the laborers who mowed your fields, which you kept back by fraud, cry out; and the cries of the harvesters have reached the ears of the Lord of hosts. [James 5:1–4]

At first it may look as if James had it in for the rich simply because they were rich. But if you look more closely, you'll see that the object of his complaint was the dirty tricks many of them employed to get where they were.

In Palestine the farm worker was really poor. He couldn't save a drachma. If he didn't get paid at the end of every day, his family had to go to bed hungry. Even so, it was apparently common practice for the wealthy landowners to defraud these poor workers out of their meager earnings. This was done in spite of the fact that it was clearly prohibited by Jewish religious law. Most people were familiar with the warning of Deuteronomy which said:

> You shall not oppress a hired servant who is poor and needy, whether he is one of your brethren or one of the sojourners who are in your land within your towns; you shall give him his hire on the day he earns it, before the sun goes down . . . lest he cry against you to the LORD, and it be sin in you. [Deut. 24:14–15]

James might have had this very passage in mind when he wrote his caustic words against the rich. But he was also familiar with the Old Testament prophets, like Isaiah and Jeremiah, who went out of their way to condemn injustice of all kinds. For instance, Isaiah had written:

> "What do you mean by crushing my people,
> by grinding the face of the poor?"
> says the Lord GOD of hosts.
> [Isa. 3:15]

The prophet Micah had flatly condemned those who cheated the poor by using undersized measures and scales that didn't weigh correctly. He had made it clear that those who got rich by deceit and fraud couldn't hope to be accepted by God. And part of their punishment was seen in the fact that with all of their wealth they couldn't find real happiness. As Micah put it: "You shall eat, but not be satisfied. . . . You shall sow, but not reap" [Micah 6:14, 15].

If James were writing to our churches today on this matter of social justice, what do you think he'd say? You can be sure he would have just as much to say about the oppression of the poor. Only, his examples would be different. He probably wouldn't mention the practice of holding back wages, because today there are strict laws against it, and the powerful labor unions see that they are enforced. But all of us know that injustice can take many forms. Just as God heard the cry of the cheated peasants in the first century, we can be sure he hears the cry of many poor people today who can't find a job because they don't have experience, and who don't have experience because they can't find a job. Furthermore, God must hear the cry of many executives who have been suddenly chopped off the payroll as a result of company mergers in which profits come first and the welfare of people comes last.

Also, the Lord hears the cry of the many migrant workers who are still badly treated in this wealthy land. Witnesses before a Senate subcommittee have left sickening stories about the subhuman treatment of thousands of migrant workers in Texas and other states. They reported that children were leaving school as soon as they were tall enough to work in the fields and that many of them were being seriously poisoned by insecticides. Vice-President Mondale summed up the situation by saying, "Wherever you find the powerless, you find a tragically disadvantaged people." True, and that's precisely the reason we've heard so much in the last few years about "black power." Here is the last hope of a depressed people for change from economic poverty to a normal share in the economic growth of our great country.

In our society some of the injustice is still done intentionally as it was in James's day. Much more of it is done unintentionally through the economic structures that we have created. An interfaith group meeting in Green Bay, Wisconsin, in September 1975 issued a report that said: "Our society's assumption has been that a competitive pursuit of private gain will work to provide the best possible life for all. Our examination of hunger in the United States convinces us that it has not provided the best possible life for all, but has resulted in exploitation of the many for the sake of the few."[24]

These are strong words, but words every American should hear. Also, we have just come through a period that has shown us how easily the best structures can be misused and corrupted. For instance, dozens of officials from government and from large corporations have been under indictment for misusing power and money. The third largest oil company in the United States dismissed its board chairman and several other top officials for using a slush fund of thirteen million dollars to help elect the political candidates of their choice. Several other companies have admitted spending even larger sums in bribes to foreign government officials. For instance, Lockheed, Northrup, Inc., admitted that two hundred million dollars went for graft and bribery in selling planes abroad.

Thank the Lord things seem to be changing. The general public is becoming more aware and more involved. Graduate schools of business in over fifty universities are planning special courses in business morality and ethics. What's more, we now know that social structures can be changed, and that Christians who work in them can be effective instruments for bringing about that change. This is the whole point of the lay ministry movement which has grown up in the last few decades. This movement has taught us that most of the hurts and most of the healing in modern society doesn't come through individuals anymore, but through systems that help or hurt, because we live in a world of organizations that determine the quality of life for all of us.

If you just stop to list all the organizations that touch your life in a single day, you'll come up with twenty-five or fifty, including many of the big ones, such as General Motors, General Electric, Exxon, and Bell Telephone. To be a Christian today means being more aware of how these organizations affect our lives and how they can and often do hurt some people. It may mean a harder look at the drug industry which realized an average of 18 percent on capital investments last year, while thirty-one other major industries realized only 9.7 percent. This may be important in relation to the number of senior citizens on fixed incomes who struggle to pay for medication.

Our interest in such things comes from our desire to build a more Christian society. If we look, we'll see that there is still plenty of injustice around us today, as there was in the first centry. As a part of our Christian discipleship, let us ask where people are being victimized, especially the poor and helpless. And let us ask what we can do to bring help and healing.

CHAPTER 14

Something to Look Forward To

"Establish your hearts, for the coming of the Lord is at hand" [James 5:8]. This also is part of James. We will do well to take it as seriously as we have tried to do with the rest of the epistle.

Admittedly, we are dealing here with something on which Christians are not agreed. At one extreme are those who write off the Second Coming of Christ as a rather childish and unscientific belief of the primitive church. At the other extreme are those who have built a complicated scheme of related events that indicate the imminent end of the world, and they are sure the time is near when they'll look up and see Jesus on a cloud.

Certainly the Christians of the first century believed that Christ would return in their generation. Our author says, "Behold, the Judge is standing at the doors" [v. 9]. Our problem is that two thousand years have passed since these words were written, and still Christ has not returned. Should we dismiss the whole matter?

We might if we could somehow do away with the many other passages in the New Testament which clearly assume that Christ is coming back to the earth. The details of this event differ somewhat from writer to writer, and even within the same book, but the conviction never waivers.

For instance, all four Gospels report Jesus urging his disciples to be ready for the great event. In some passages, such as Matt., ch. 24, it is easy to confuse final things with the description of the fall of Jerusalem. But it is clear that Jesus taught his disciples that he would return. The church has preserved the important words "till he come" as a reminder in the service of Communion.

The epistles of Paul are also quite positive on the Second Coming. The passage in First Thessalonians is one of the best known:

> For the Lord himself will descend from heaven with a cry of command, with the archangel's call, and with the sound of the trumpet of God . . . . For you yourselves know well that the day of the Lord will come. [I Thess. 4:16; 5:2]

The book of Revelation, which is a vision of God's final victory, ends with the words of the risen Lord, "Surely I am coming soon" [Rev. 22:20].

So the New Testament is consistent in teaching that Christ will return. It is also consistent in telling us that no man knows the day or the hour. It should therefore come as no real shock to learn that the first-century Christians were mistaken in thinking they would live to see it. Through the centuries others have been equally confident, some using numerology for their predictions, others the position of the planets, and some even the dimensions of the pyramids!

The Millerites thought the Lord was going to return on October 22, 1844, and waited in white robes on hills and rooftops. Today there seem to be an ever-increasing number of groups who believe the Lord will return in our generation. For proof, they point their finger at social, economic, and moral conditions of our time which seem to match the forecasts of the New Testament. One writer explains:

> In the last days of this church age, there will be bitter contention between the rich and the poor, between capi-

tal and labor, accompanied by so much cruel oppression, so much wanton wickedness, that divine intervention will become imperative.[25]

This is a strong personal conviction, but still a human judgment. And who is to say that contention between the classes, cruel oppression, and wanton wickedness are any worse today than they were in some other periods of history or will be at yet some future time?

Furthermore, such conditions are never the same all over the world. They differ greatly from place to place even within the same country. So it is still true that no man knows the day or the hour when the Son of Man will return.

The second thing that is clear on this subject is that Christians must live expectantly. Jesus taught that we should be like a conscientious servant who never knows when his master will come home, but is always ready for his coming [Matt: 24:36–51]. Long delay should never lead one to carelessness or despair. Today we need the word of Jesus on patience even more than did the Christians of the first century.

The third thing the New Testament makes clear is that a part of the preparation of Christians for the Second Coming is to be sure they are living in fellowship with their Christian brothers and sisters. James says simply that members of the church must not complain about one another [James 5:9].

Clear enough. But what about the imagery—the blast of the trumpet, Christ on a cloud, and the multitude of angels? James says nothing about these particulars, and most of us will do well to follow his example.

It is much more meaningful for most of us to think of the Second Coming in the cosmic sense which Paul wrote about in his Ephesian letter.

For he has made known to us in all wisdom and insight the mystery of his will, according to his purpose which he set forth in Christ as a plan for the fulness of time, to unite all things in him, things in heaven and things on earth. [Eph. 1: 9–10]

Here is stated the Biblical faith that history does not move in endless circles. Rather, it moves ever closer to the day when all things will find their meaning and unity in Christ. This means that even now God is working in human history toward the final unity and harmony of all things in Christ. The title of a book by J. A. T. Robinson catches the idea perfectly. It is called *In the End God.*

God is now creating the end of history just as surely as he created the beginning. One of the world's greatest anthropologists, Pierre Teilhard de Chardin, writes: "The world is only interesting when one looks forward." He argues that the final extinction of man would destroy the very meaning of evolution and that since the world's very existence has proved a hundred times over to be a reasoned process, it is not thinkable that all this could come to a senseless end in absolute death. He concludes with this amazing statement:

Man's future is obviously a higher centralization of his spiritual substance around one point.[26]

The apostles would say, "That point is none other than Jesus Christ!"

So, today we are living between the times, between the two advents of our Lord, in what the New Testament calls "the last days." Some Christians are reluctant to talk about the Second Coming because it sometimes becomes for those who appear to take it most seriously an escape from responsibility. But it *can* produce just the opposite kind of motivation.

U Kyaw Than, a former colleague of mine in Burma, tells of once discussing this matter with the great Swiss theologian, Karl Barth. At one point Kyaw Than asked Barth if belief in the Second Coming didn't make Christians resigned and complacent. The reply was quick and clear. Barth said:

How could a servant expecting any moment the return of the master remain inactive and complacent? He would be all the more active, using every moment to prepare for the master's arrival! He would be asking: "What has the master told me to do? Have I done it?"

This is precisely the question each of us should be asking ourselves. Someday, perhaps soon, the Master will return. What has he asked me to do? And have I done it?

CHAPTER 15

The Caring Community

When we Americans moved from the farm to the city, we lost something. Not just the old wooden churn and fresh buttermilk, but the feeling of community and the family kind of concern about one another which tied us all together.

Today our society is woefully fragmented. The Christian church may well be the last remnant of closeness where we still rejoice with those who rejoice and weep with those who weep.

James gave us a remarkable picture of what the early church was like, and what any church can be today. In the fifth chapter, the thirteenth verse, we find these words:

Is any one among you suffering? Let him pray. Is any cheerful? Let him sing praise. Is any among you sick? Let him call for the elders of the church, and let them pray over him, anointing him with oil in the name of the Lord; and the prayer of faith will save the sick man, and the Lord will raise him up; and if he has committed sins, he will be forgiven. Therefore confess your sins to one another, . . . that you may be healed. [James 5:13–16]

Note first, James assumes that the church should be a fellowship of prayer. He runs through the whole catalog of human emotions—sorrow, joy, sickness, guilt—and concludes that it is prayer which should undergird and enrich every experience. That's the way it should be.

But what has gone wrong? Today many people have stopped praying, and you don't even hear much about prayer in some churches. Still more serious is a report by the religion editor of *The New York Times* that "many clergymen frankly state . . . they no longer bother to pray." Whatever the excuse for this strange development, you can be sure it is most serious, because prayer is the very heartbeat of the Christian faith. And it still makes a difference.

Prayer should be used in all of life's circumstances. For instance, James says: "Is any one among you suffering? Let him pray" [James 5:13]. The word "suffering" used here could mean any kind of distress, including what we today call anxiety and depression. Prayer puts us in touch with the power of God, which can quickly bring a sense of release and fulfillment.

Next, James says: "Is any cheerful? Let him sing praise" [v. 13]. Music, too, has an important place in the ministry of the church and should not be the first thing to be cut from the budget. Music is a way of thinking in tones and expressing otherwise hidden feelings. This is especially true of the feelings of gratitude and praise. Our oldest hymns are psalms, and our spiritual ancestors, the Puritans, insisted that these were the only hymns suitable for Christian worship. Let's be thankful their limited view didn't prevail and that today we can rejoice with our young people as they sing Christian folk songs and modern music such as that of Avery and Marsh accompanied by guitars and drums. The church should be a community in which happy people can share their joy. The songs of praise provide an opportunity for the whole congregation to say: "Praise the Lord. We're glad with you."

Next, James says: "Is any among you sick?" Your fellow church members care about this too. Such caring goes back to Jesus himself, who was moved with compassion by the sick and suffering of his day. He often went out of his way to restore a blind or lame person to health. Unlike Buddhists and Hindus, Christians have never accepted human suffering as the intentional will of God, but have always believed that God wanted his children to be made whole. Such wholeness is inherent in the meaning of the word "salvation." So Christians have built hospitals, carried on medical research, and sent doctors to every part of the globe.

And this is not all they have done. Since the days of the apostles, they have prayed for God to heal the sick, and have often seen their prayers answered in miraculous ways. A grateful friend of mine said recently, "My church simply loved me back to health." James suggests a particular formula for healing services. He writes, "Call for the elders of the church, and let them pray over him, anointing him with oil" [James 5:14].

The "elders" were the lay leaders of the early church and not necessarily "senior citizens." The title referred to their office, not to their age. Together they represented the spiritual authority of the community. In some denominations of the Reformed tradition, "elders" are still elected to serve as the chief ruling body of the church. The most comparable role in other churches would be that of deacon. Whatever they may be called, James presents a picture of the church becoming a healing community through prayer.

We have gone through a period in recent years in which scientism caused many to discredit the possibility of divine healing. For some, the motto "In God We Trust" was revised to read, "In Science We Trust." Only gradually have we moved to a more balanced position. There is now increasing evidence that the gap between science and religion is being bridged. For instance, when the hospital chapel in our community was dedicated, it was the mayor who spoke at considerable length about the importance of spiritual factors in healing. Furthermore, the American Medical Association now has a Department of Medicine and Religion which has issued this statement: "Medical leaders recognize that man cannot be separated into parts for care and treatment of illness. Man is a whole being. His health is affected by physical, spiritual, emotional and social factors. . . . The faith of the individual patient is a vital factor to total health."[27]

Along with this are a number of studies that prove that many people are healed by a power beyond medical science. For instance, Dr. P. Collipp, chief of pediatrics at Nassau County Medical Center in New York, reports that a recent study of his supports the view that prayer does make a difference. In my own church, I asked one Sunday if any were afflicted and believed that God wanted to heal them. An elderly woman walked to the chancel steps and explained she had suffered for months from severe whiplash. We placed our hands on her head and prayed that God would touch her. Later, I was eating dinner when the phone rang. A very grateful woman said: "I've been healed. The pain is gone and I can move my head as freely as before."

This shouldn't surprise any of us. For the heart of God has not changed. He wants all his children to be healthy and whole. He can still heal anything from a broken nose to a broken heart. So let's put healing into the caring ministry of the church, where it belongs. And while we're at it, let's not think of healing only in physical terms. To be sure, sin is not the cause of every illness, but where it is present, this roadblock must be removed.

Our Scripture next moves into something else which should characterize the church. James says, "Confess your sins to one another, . . . that you may be healed." The Moravian Church has had a long history of members confessing sins to one another. John Wesley took over the practice for his weekly class meetings. Surely such a practice requires a special community of love where people feel they can share openly and honestly without being ostracized. Unfortunately, many of our churches aren't quite making it. Because of a judgmental rather than a forgiving spirit the church is for many of its members the last place they would openly confess their sins. This must change if we are to be the kind of caring community God intended.

Finally, we know that God cares for each of us, and he expects us to care for each other. Such caring isn't easy. This kind of caring requires that we enter into both the joy and the hurts of the other person. To care means to share both the blessings and the burdens. To do so takes courage, and there is always a risk factor. Some people don't want others too close. So, we may get the door slammed in our face. But there is also the possibility of seeing the door open and discovering a new high in human relationships through mutual trust and support.

Let us thank God for a caring community in which we can sing, "Blest be the tie that binds our hearts in Christian love."

CHAPTER **16**

Something to Live By

The question we asked in the first chapter is with us to the
last. What is God's word to us through the words found in
The Epistle of James? On the basis of our own reading, each
of us would sum it up differently, but surely none of us can
leave out the following:

—Right and wrong are written into the very nature of
human existence and are not altered by modern opinion polls.

—God still uses the hard places of life to build strong
character and bring us closer to himself.

—All of us need true wisdom, and it is never farther than
a prayer away.

—Material possessions can rob us of life's greatest treasures.

—It is time to stop blaming God or the devil for our moral
failures and admit that we are responsible.

—Undisciplined temper simply has no place in the Christian life-style.

—Though salvation can never be earned by good works,
the quality of one's daily life is always the final test of
faith.

—Our tongue is a small but powerful instrument. We must
learn to use it for honest communication and the up-
building of others.

—The world's status symbols are meaningless in God's

sight. Everybody is of immeasurable value to him.
—When we make plans that leave God out, we betray our sinful arrogance.
—Sin comes in all shapes and sizes and may be simply a matter of failing to do something when we know very well it should be done.
—Sometimes life may seem to move in circles, but it is important to know that it always has divine direction and is ever nearer that day when God will sum up all things in Christ.
—In our age of conflicting interests the Christian church can and must be the demonstration point of real community.

All of this, and more, we have discovered in The Epistle of James—a handful of pearls indeed.

And who is sufficient for these things? Surely none of us by ourselves. "But he gives more grace" [James 4:6].

NOTES

1. Martin Luther, *Luther's Works* (Muhlenberg Press, Publishers, 1960), Vol. 35, p. 362.

2. Edgar J. Goodspeed, *An Introduction to the New Testament* (The University of Chicago Press, 1937), p. 290.

3. Rabbi Seymour Siegel, in *The Milwaukee Journal,* Jan. 15, 1977.

4. Helen Keller, in *Atlantic* monthly, Jan. 1933, p. 35.

5. Melvin E. Schoonover, *Letters to Polly: On the Gift of Affliction* (Wm. B. Eerdmans Publishing Co., 1971), p. 29.

6. Robert S. Brown, in *Family Circle,* March 1976.

7. Christmas Humphreys, *Buddhism* (Penguin Books, 1955), p. 21.

8. Gen. 3:5.

9. Leonard Bernstein *et al., West Side Story* (Random House, Inc., 1967), p. 117.

10. Thomas Jefferson, A Decalogue of Canons for Observation in Practical Life, Feb. 21, 1825.

11. Mark Twain, *Pudd'nhead Wilson* (1894). *Pudd'nhead Wilson's Calendar,* ch. 10.

12. Homer, *The Odyssey,* Book I.

13. *The Interpreter's Bible* (Abingdon Press, 1957), Vol. 12, p. 35.

14. Charles Wells, *Between the Lines,* Jan. 1976.

15. Robert Burns, *The Complete Poetical Works of Burns* (Houghton, 1897).

16. William Barclay, *The Letters of James and Peter,* The

Daily Study Bible Series (The Westminster Press, 1960), p. 92.

17. Arnold Toynbee, *Look* magazine, Aug. 17, 1948, p. 23.

18. Margaret J. Anderson, *The Christian Writer's Handbook* (Harper & Row, Publishers, 1974), p. 78.

19. *The Interpreter's Bible* (Abingdon Press, 1957), Vol. 12, p. 49.

20. Reinhold Niebuhr, *Beyond Tragedy* (Charles Scribner's Sons, 1937), p. 17.

21. *Ibid.,* p. 100.

22. George Bernard Shaw, *The Devil's Disciple,* Act II.

23. William Barclay, *The Letters of James and Peter,* The Daily Study Bible Series (The Westminster Press, 1960), p. 138.

24. *The Cleveland Press,* Sept. 20, 1975, p. A6.

25. Murray Downey, *James, A Practical Faith* (Moody Press, 1972), p. 80.

26. Joseph V. Kopp, *Teilhard de Chardin: A New Synthesis of Evolution* (Paulist Press, 1963).

27. American Medical Association, a brochure.